BUT WHAT ABOUT GOD'S WRATH?

THE COMPELLING LOVE STORY OF DIVINE ANGER

KEVIN KINGHORN

with

STEPHEN TRAVIS

IVP Academic

An imprint of InterVarsity Press
Downers Grove, Illinois

InterVarsity Press
P.O. Box 1400, Downers Grove, IL 60515-1426
ivpress.com
email@ivpress.com

InterVarsity Press® is the book-publishing division of InterVarsity Christian Fellowship/USA®, a movement of
students and faculty active on campus at hundreds of universities, colleges, and schools of nursing in the United
States of America, and a member movement of the International Fellowship of Evangelical Students. For
information about local and regional activities, visit intervarsity.org.

Cover design and image composite: David Fassett
Interior design: Daniel van Loon
Images: plants growing in the dark: © Sven Krobot / EyeEm / Getty Images
        knife-scratched paper: © MirageC / Moment Collection / Getty Images
        watercolor paper texture: © Dmytro Synelnychenkon / iStock / Getty Images Plus

ISBN 978-0-8308-5229-1 (print)
ISBN 978-0-8308-7367-8 (digital)

Printed in the United States of America ∞

InterVarsity Press is committed to ecological stewardship and to the conservation of natural resources in all our
operations. This book was printed using sustainably sourced paper.

Library of Congress Cataloging-in-Publication Data

Names: Kinghorn, Kevin Paul, 1967- author.
Title: But what about God's wrath? : the compelling love story of divine
    anger / Kevin Kinghorn, with Stephen Travis.
Description: Westmont : InterVarsity Press, 2019. | Includes
    bibliographical references and index.
Identifiers: LCCN 2019031164 (print) | LCCN 2019031165 (ebook) | ISBN
    9780830852291 (paperback) | ISBN 9780830873678 (ebook)
Subjects: LCSH: God (Christianity)—Love. | God (Christianity)—Wrath.
Classification: LCC BT140 .K56 2019 (print) | LCC BT140 (ebook) | DDC
    231/.6—dc23
LC record available at https://lccn.loc.gov/2019031164
LC ebook record available at https://lccn.loc.gov/2019031165

| P | 25 | 24 | 23 | 22 | 21 | 20 | 19 | 18 | 17 | 16 | 15 | 14 | 13 | 12 | 11 | 10 | 9 | 8 | 7 | 6 | 5 | 4 | 3 | 2 | 1 |
| Y | 37 | 36 | 35 | 34 | 33 | 32 | 31 | 30 | 29 | 28 | 27 | 26 | 25 | 24 | 23 | 22 | 21 | 20 | 19 |

For Ken and Hilda,

whose parenting never gave me any reason to doubt

God's persistent love for us.

CONTENTS

ACKNOWLEDGMENTS

Although I am the single writer of this book, the ideas within it are most definitely co-authored. Stephen Travis provided 150 pages (single spaced!) of systematic notes on biblical passages having to do with God's wrath. His biblical scholarship has been so incredibly valuable, both in terms of analyzing individual passages and in terms of understanding broader themes within the biblical narrative. His notes and comments not only helped shape this book, but have also helped me, more widely, appreciate the devotional richness of parts of the Bible I had previously thought of as tough reading. Above all, he has been an encourager throughout the stages of this project and a joy to count as a colleague.

The bulk of the writing for this project was completed during a sabbatical from Asbury Theological Seminary, whose generosity I greatly appreciate. I am indebted to the editors at IVP, particularly Anna Gissing, for improvements to this manuscript, along with an anonymous reviewer. Thanks to members of my weekly reading group—Nick Grounds, Dylan Ziegler, Robert Williams, Evan Drysdale, Corban McKain, and Derek King—for providing helpful feedback in discussions of the topic. Thanks to Seth Sizemore for reading an early version of the manuscript and for suggested issues to address. Thanks to Jerry Walls for his initial encouragement to write this book. Finally, thanks to my wife, Barbara, and children, Anna Keren and Joseph, for their continued support of this and every other project of mine.

INTRODUCTION

There's a sticking point that arises again and again in my conversations with many Christians over the years. We'll be talking about the character of God, the significance of the cross, the nature of faith, salvation, and so on. We'll be talking about God's great love for us, his desire that we live abundantly, and his efforts to draw people to himself. It's great theological conversation among fellow believers. But then the sticking point arises.

I myself am in the broad Wesleyan tradition, and many of these conversations have been with fellow Christians who come from a more Reformed theological background. They join me in affirming God's great love for us. But at a certain point, when drawing out what I think are the implications from this starting point that God is love, they caution me as follows. "So far we've only been speaking about God's *love*. But what about God's *wrath*?"

There's a lot in Scripture about God's love for us. But there's quite a lot about God's wrath as well. Is God's love only one side of God's character? Is wrath really another, complementary side we must consider? Paul tells us in Romans 11:22 to consider the "kindness and sternness of God." In another translation it's the "goodness and severity of God" (KJV). Would it therefore be a weak, tepid, overly feel-good theology that considers only God's love but neglects to consider God's wrath?

This book explores the relationship between God's love and God's wrath. It does so using two approaches. I myself am a Christian philosopher, and the eight chapters of this book make up a single, sustained line of argument for the conclusion that God's wrath is entirely an expression of God's love, in specific contexts. And all the ways God relates to us—including his expressions of wrath—can be derived from the starting point of God's love.

The second approach in this book is one of biblical studies. I have worked with biblical scholar Stephen Travis on this project, drawing from his insightful, extended notes on how God's wrath is understood within the biblical narrative. This book can be described as the outcome of a philosopher and a biblical scholar putting their heads together. Stephen and I end up with the same conclusion about the relationship God's love has to God's wrath. His approach is a careful review of the biblical texts. My own approach is to carefully draw out the implications of certain starting points that all Christians will agree on. The eight chapters are, as I said, structured as a philosophical line of argument. But along the way there is equal attention paid to biblical themes and to contextual study, which informs the discussion and moves it forward.

Most, if not all, theological disagreements stem ultimately from differing ways of understanding God's nature and character. As small children we all wanted to embrace the idea that God is love. This is super simple theology. But a more mature theology recognizes that God's revelation about his character is more complex. It involves themes of his justice, his judgment, at times his wrath. We must go deeper in our theology than a five-year-old's simplistic picture of God. Yet, what if a deeper biblical and philosophical analysis of God's character actually leads us back once again to that simple—though this time not simplistic—understanding that God is love?

1

WRATH AS A PATTERN OF ACTION

In the age before tablets and cell phones, families would often pass the time on long car trips by playing the game "Twenty Questions." That game always begins with the initial question: Is it an animal, vegetable, or mineral? Similarly, any analysis of God's wrath needs to start by clarifying what *wrath* refers to. Is it an emotion? A disposition? An action? Something else?

WRATH AND THE EMOTION OF ANGER

An answer here is not immediately obvious. This is because the term *wrath* can be used to denote a variety of occurrences in Scripture. One kind of repeated reference to wrath seems pretty plainly to refer to an *emotion*. Consider, for instance, Proverbs 15:1: "A gentle answer turns away wrath, but a harsh word stirs up anger." The context here seems to be how a gentle answer soothes the emotion of wrath. First Kings 14:22 indicates that God's wrath can indeed be "stirred up." Similarly, Jeremiah 32:32 tells how the people's actions have "provoked" the Lord. Yet again, we read in Deuteronomy 9:8 that "at Horeb you aroused the LORD's wrath so that he was angry enough to destroy you." This is language one naturally associates with the rising and falling of an emotion. *Wrath* in these contexts might be thought of as a synonym for "feeling angry."

We could substitute other English words here besides *anger*. In English we have a variety of words that point to similar kinds of emotional states: *displeasure, annoyance, resentment, rage, fury,* and so forth. In Hebrew too there are a variety of words for this general kind of emotional reaction, which the Old Testament uses in describing both humans and God. Although it would be possible in English and in Hebrew to trace out all the subtle differences among these related terms, for our purposes there is no need to do so. The point remains that God is frequently described in Scripture as having emotions associated with anger or wrath.

The term *wrath* seems often to be the preferred choice of people today when talking about this angry side of God we see in Scripture. Otherwise, though, in everyday speech it is rarely used. It is a bit like the English word *ire*. You may know what the term means, but when was the last time you used *ire* in a conversation? So it is with discussions about God's wrath. There is nothing unique about the term. I will use it in this book to refer generally to God's anger or expressed displeasure, as depicted in Scripture.

It is actually a great irony that the term *wrath* has become something of a special theological term for God's anger or displeasure. The irony is that the biblical use of the term is specifically *not* intended for the context of abstract, academic discussions. References to God's wrath are meant to convey the intensity of God's reaction to real-life situations. They convey God's rage, his fury, as he relates to humans in our world, made messy by injustice, oppression, and human suffering.

Some people are surprised to find the Bible using such words as *fury* or *wrath* to describe God. They think of such language as crude or primitive, not suitable for a mature and enlightened conversation about the character of God. But the biblical language—particularly the Old Testament Hebrew—is direct, vivid, earthy. Centuries later, Christian writers in the early church drew from the more abstract and sophisticated language of Greek and Roman thought. They made subtle theological distinctions using such terms as *Trinity, substance,* and *essence.* But the Hebrew language in particular speaks with a much greater vibrancy. Using this language, biblical writers emphasize God's aliveness, his character as someone who loves, cares, acts, feels joy and regret and anguish as we do.

I do not, of course, mean that God is just like us. God is infinitely greater than we are. But the Bible's vivid language of human emotion is the best way for us to see that God cares about us and that we can relate to him. After all, we humans are emotional beings. Our strong reaction to a harmful event includes our emotional reaction. If I witnessed a friend having no emotional reaction to a dramatic movie, I would conclude that he was just not moved by the subject matter.

It seems impossible to imagine how we could understand a revelation from God of his personal interest in us, if emotional language were not part of that revelation. *Wrath* is part of the emotional language used in the Bible to convey the care God has for us. Just as we, at our best, react strongly and purposefully when someone we care about is mistreated or when justice is undermined, so does the God of the Bible. God is not like a judge in a courthouse, suspending his personal feelings in order to act objectively. He is more like a parent who feels affronted when her daughter is bullied in school and who takes steps to confront the offender.

THE PLACE OF RIGHTEOUS ANGER

This example of an enraged parent helps make the point that an emotion associated with wrath can be completely legitimate. We sometimes refer to it as *righteous anger.* A virtuous response to instances of injustice and oppression *should* include righteous anger. If you were to witness a marginalized person being exploited by someone in power, and if your reaction weren't one of righteous anger, then questions could surely be asked about your moral character. How could you be oriented toward the good, toward the fullness of life that God intends for people, and *not* be unsettled and outraged by cruelty, scandal, and sin of all kinds?

God's anger as legitimate jealousy for people's affection. Sometimes the biblical accounts of God's anger take the form of God's *jealousy*. We read, for example, in Deuteronomy 32:16 that God's people "made him jealous with their foreign gods, and angered him with their detestable idols." Admittedly, jealousy for someone else's affection can sometimes be unwarranted and destructive. For example, a husband might be improperly controlling of his wife, demanding to know her every movement and becoming furious if she even looks at a stranger. Or a woman might stalk an ex-boyfriend and try to secretly undermine any subsequent relationship he tries to form.

All the same, at other times jealousy for someone else's affection can be wholly justified. A husband and wife pledge at their wedding ceremony to be faithful to each other. If one spouse then grows unduly attached to someone else, the other spouse is right to have the kind of righteous anger we associate with jealousy. In this context, feelings of jealousy are entirely appropriate. Something would be wrong if a spouse *didn't* feel jealousy for the unique affection that was pledged at the wedding ceremony.

The Bible in a number of places describes God as in this sense a jealous God for his people. God is recorded in Exodus 34:14 as warning his people against worshiping other gods, "for the Lord, whose name is Jealous, is a jealous God." In the New Testament, Paul writes of sharing in this same kind of jealousy: "I am jealous for you with a godly jealousy. I promised you to one husband, to Christ, so that I might present you as a pure virgin to him" (2 Corinthians 11:2).

Just as legitimate jealousy can exist within the relationship of husband and wife, it can exist within other kinds of relationships as well. Hosea 11:1-9 vividly portrays God as a mother who feels betrayed by her child, Israel. She has cherished him, taught him to walk, given herself to his growth and development. But he has rebelled against her and rejected the values she taught him by chasing after the Baals (Canaanite gods).

God's anger at people's mistreatment of others. Another biblical context of God's righteous anger involves the harm that one person does to another, especially to those on the margins of society. God is the one who warns his people that "my anger will be aroused" if they "take advantage of the widow or the fatherless" (Exodus 22:22, 24). For a God who values justice and righteousness, disregard of the laws designed to safeguard the poor and vulnerable is a serious offense. In Isaiah 5:8-30 we find a series of woes in which God denounces the powerful people such as landowners who take advantage of poor farmers forced to sell their land because of accumulated debts—contravening the laws of Leviticus 25:23-28, 35-43. The book of Isaiah also contains God's well-known complaint against the worship and fasting of his people: "On the day of your fasting, you do as you please and exploit all your workers" (Isaiah 58:3). For this reason God has turned away from them, declaring, "You cannot fast as you do today and expect your voice to be heard on high" (Isaiah 58:4). God then explains to the people what they should already know:

> Is not this the kind of fasting I have chosen:
>
> to loose the chains of injustice
> and untie the cords of the yoke,
>
> to set the oppressed free
> and break every yoke?
>
> Is it not to share your food with the hungry
> and to provide the poor wanderer with shelter—
>
> when you see the naked, to clothe them,
> and not to turn away from your own flesh and blood? (Isaiah 58:6-7)

Turning to the New Testament, Jesus' own recorded instances of righteous anger typically involve this same context of people impeding the well-being of others. We read in Mark of a Sabbath when Jesus is in the synagogue, along with a man with a paralyzed hand (Mark 3:1-6). Critics of Jesus watch intently to see whether he will attempt to heal the paralysis—which in their view would count as forbidden work on the Sabbath. "Then Jesus asked them, 'Which is lawful on the Sabbath: to do good or to do evil, to save life or to kill?' But they remained silent. He looked around at them in anger and, deeply distressed at their stubborn hearts, said to the man, 'Stretch out your hand.' He stretched it out, and his hand was completely restored" (Mark 3:4-5). Jesus is angry that people would use the Sabbath law to prohibit doing good to someone in need.

Jesus' anger is notably focused on those who hinder the flourishing of children. In Mark 10:13-14 we read of a time in which "people were bringing little children to Jesus for him to place his hands on them, but the disciples rebuked them. When Jesus saw this, he was indignant. He said to them, 'Let the little children come to me, and do not hinder them, for the kingdom of God belongs to such as these.'" The word *indignant* is not a mild response, in the language of the New Testament. It is the same reaction the chief priests and teachers of the law are recorded in Matthew 21:15 as having at hearing children shouting "Hosanna to the Son of David" after Jesus cleansed the temple and healed sick people there.

Perhaps the starkest expression of Jesus' righteous anger within the New Testament is found in Matthew 18:6. After picking out a little child who is present, Jesus remarks, "If anyone causes one of these little ones—those who believe in me—to stumble, it would be better for them to have a large millstone hung around their neck and to be drowned in the depths of the sea."

So there are plenty of examples in Scripture of God's anger being directed toward those who harm others. In addition, a large set of examples can be found of God's anger directed at those who bring harm on themselves. This context for God's wrath is worth considering carefully.

God's anger at people's self-destructive behavior. This context of God's angry reaction to people's self-destructive tendencies is an over-arching context throughout the whole narrative of Scripture. Even where God's anger is linked with his jealousy, we also find this element of being troubled, being angry, for our sake. Jeremiah 7:18-19 makes this point explicitly: "'They pour out drink offerings to other gods to arouse my anger. But am I the one they are provoking?' declares the LORD. 'Are they not rather harming themselves, to their own shame?'" (see also Jeremiah 25:7). In damaging our relationship with God, we cut ourselves off from the one source of fullness of life. A God who cares about us would naturally be troubled, for *our* sake, at our sins against him.

In the New Testament as well we find God troubled by people's self-destructive tendencies. A clear example is Jesus' lament over Jerusalem: "Jerusalem, Jerusalem, you who kill the prophets and stone those sent to you, how often I have longed to gather your children together, as a hen gathers her chicks under her wings, and you were not willing" (Matthew 23:37). Would God's feeling of lament mix with anger, in the context of his concern for us? The clear answer to this seems to be yes—if our own experiences as parents are any guide to how God reacts to seeing his loved ones act in self-destructive ways.

For parents, it is worth reflecting on the anger we can sometimes feel when our children put themselves in danger. Especially when we have warned our children about the hazards of some activity, seeing our children then endanger themselves can cause powerful emotions in us. Some toddlers, for instance, seem to have an enthusiasm for running toward parking lots and other areas where there is traffic. A parent of a toddler once confided to me, "I can't believe the level of rage I experience when my child runs toward the street." Of course, it is entirely appropriate for parents to feel a kind of protective anger. There would be something wrong if parents' strong emotions *weren't* aroused when the safety of their children was at stake.

This same protective anger is a strong, overarching theme throughout the biblical references to God's anger. It is interesting to note the pattern of God's wrath within the Old Testament. Nearly always this wrath is directed toward God's own people, Israel. (Only later in the Old Testament, and with fewer references, is God's wrath directed toward other nations.) These are the people whom he has specially promised to guide and care for. His anger at their rebellious ways comes in the context of his constant striving to renew them as his cherished people.

When the Bible attributes wrath or anger to God, it is not describing a God whose rage is like the tantrums of a three-year-old, or a God who flies off the handle like a boss whose employee has yet again ruined a work project. God's anger is not an uncontrolled emotion. It is instead more like the controlled anger of a parent whose teenage daughter has stayed out way beyond the expected time of her return home and has thereby not only worried her parents but also made herself vulnerable to unwelcome dangers. Such anger is motivated by concern for the well-being of the person toward whom it is directed. It expresses disapproval within a context of care and concern, and it aims at a more responsible and trusting relationship moving forward.

Anger in this context can still be intense. The Bible's depiction of God includes God reacting passionately, furiously, when his people fail to respond to the avenues toward healing and restoration that he himself is providing. Again thinking of our own human experiences, anger seems an entirely appropriate emotion when we witness others' failures to take advantage of opportunities that life affords them. We humans get exasperated when others—especially those we've invested in deeply—squander chances and fail to live up to their potential. We lament such things, often exclaiming, "What a waste!" This feeling of lament is often mixed with frustration, with anger, as we reflect on the good things that might have been but are not.

In subsequent chapters I will have more to say about how God's wrath really is best seen as falling under the umbrella of care and concern for those who are the objects of wrath. But for now it is worth noting how the three contexts for God's wrath, as outlined in this section, are not competing contexts. These three contexts are by no means mutually exclusive, and indeed they work in conjunction with one another.

Consider again the passage from Jeremiah 7 in which God is "provoked to anger" as his people "pour out drink offerings to other gods" and in the process "harm themselves." It is not just that people have spurned God by taking up with other gods, thereby breaking their pledge to be faithful to him. It is not just that God is angry at their self-destructive behavior. Jeremiah also includes the point that their unfaithfulness is impeding God's desire to bring blessing to the nations (Jeremiah 4:2). We see clearly these three concerns that motivate God's anger: that his people be faithful to him, that they flourish as he had always intended them to flourish, and that they serve as instruments to bring life to others.

Any wrong action inevitably undercuts all three of these purposes. We humans recognize this in everyday examples. We become angry and frustrated with friends or family members who relapse in their recovery from addiction of some kind. We recognize the behavior as self-destructive, and we recognize the impact it has on others around them. Plus, we feel a bit betrayed because they had promised us they would not repeat this pattern. Or consider the outrage we feel when a factory worker blithely ignores safety rules, putting himself and his coworkers in danger—not to mention violating the public trust we all pledge to uphold by agreeing to have safety laws in the first place. As with any act of wrongdoing, a person's own long-term welfare will be compromised, along with the well-being of others, and someone's trust will be violated.

These three, related concerns are again seen in Jesus' most demonstrative expression of anger: his cleansing of the temple in Jerusalem, recorded in Mark 11:15-18. We read of him "driving out those who were buying and selling there. He overturned the tables of the money changers and the benches of those selling doves, and would not allow anyone to carry merchandise through the temple courts" (Mark 11:15-16). Jesus' stated concern is of course that God's house be a "house of prayer for all nations" and not a "den of robbers" (Mark 11:17). This speaks to God's legitimate jealousy that his purposes in establishing this holy place should be honored and not perverted. But Jesus' actions are also part of his larger pattern of protesting the failure of Israel's leaders to guide the people in a way that is true to God's intentions. The leaders had made religion an obstacle for the people rather than a signpost to the living God. Thus Jesus' reaction at the temple is partly explained by his anger at the way people have impeded the flourishing of others. Finally, all of Jesus' teachings contain the ever-present warning that, for our own sakes, we should be careful not to cause others to stumble, or to call them fools, or to sin in any way against them—for these are the self-destructive paths that lead to hell (see Matthew 5:21-30).

In sum, the Bible depicts God as having strong emotional responses of anger or wrath. We need not shy away from attributing this emotion to God. Perhaps for humans the emotion of anger is often associated with an uncontrolled outburst or a failure to engage in thoughtful decision-making. We sometimes speak of our tempers getting the better of us, resulting in times when we are far from our best. But this is decidedly *not* the biblical context for affirming God's emotional response of anger or wrath. A careful study of the Scriptures shows a God who cares passionately about people and who is deeply distressed and angered when people are harmed by others and by their own self-destructive actions.

WHY GOD'S WRATH IS MORE THAN AN EMOTION

In the remainder of this chapter I want to discuss why a focus on emotions does not actually have the potential to give us an ultimate explanation of God's wrath. Put another way, expressions of divine wrath cannot be adequately analyzed or explained by appealing to an emotion. If one asks, "What explains this instance of God's wrath?" the answer cannot be, "Because a feeling of righteous anger arose in God."

Why is an angry emotion an inadequate explanation of God's wrath? Consider that the biblical references to God's wrath are commonly references to God doing something, to God acting in some way. Divine wrath is often described as coming on or falling on individuals and groups (e.g., Numbers 1:53; 18:5; Joshua 22:20; 2 Chronicles 19:2; Zephaniah 2:2). God's wrath can break out against others (2 Samuel 6:8). It is something that is poured out on others (Psalm 79:6; Jeremiah 10:25; 42:18; Ezekiel 36:18; Hosea 5:10; Revelation 16:1).

God's wrath is sometimes linked with setting accounts straight: "According to what they have done, so will he repay wrath to his enemies and retribution to his foes" (Isaiah 59:18). The actions associated with divine wrath can at times be carried out by others: "I have summoned my warriors to carry out my wrath" (Isaiah 13:3). Indeed, penalties may await those who fail to carry out divine directives associated with God's wrath: "Because you did not obey the LORD or carry out his fierce wrath against the Amalekites, the LORD has done this to you today" (1 Samuel 28:18).

The focus of Paul's discussions of divine wrath is likewise God's active judgment on sin. God's wrath is directed toward unbelievers on account of their "godlessness and wickedness" (Romans 1:18). Of course a dominant theme of Revelation is the final judgment, which is linked again and again to God's wrath. The time when God's "wrath has come" is linked with "the time" for "judging the dead" (Revelation 11:18). To be judged as unrighteous is to "drink the wine of God's fury, which has been poured full strength into the cup of his wrath" (Revelation 14:10). Or, in a similar image, final judgment is represented by being thrown into the great "winepress of God's wrath" (Revelation 14:19). This final judgment prompts the warning John the Baptist gives early in the Gospels as part of his call to repentance: "You brood of vipers! Who warned you to flee from the coming wrath?" (Luke 3:7).

These references are to God doing something: settling accounts, pronouncing judgment, punishing, extinguishing, and the like. An attempt to understand divine wrath by focusing on an emotion (such as righteous anger) thus seems inadequate. An emotion is a far different thing from an action. Often times, we may experience a certain emotion—anger, sadness, disappointment, joy, satisfaction—and not do anything. We simply experience the emotion. Thus, noting that God has an emotion we might describe as righteous anger does not yet account for the way wrath is so often linked in Scripture with an action God performs.

Emotions can move us some way toward an action when they are accompanied by a desire to act in some way. For example, if someone is dissatisfied with her job, she may naturally have a desire to search actively for a new one. Admittedly, most all the biblical references to God's righteous anger are naturally read as also including a desire to do something about the situation that angers God.

Nevertheless, a desire to act is itself still not an action. A person may have a desire to phone a colleague who is going through a difficult time. But he may judge that the timing is not right, and in the end perhaps he refrains from phoning at the moment. Having a desire in no way guarantees that one will act on that desire. Accordingly, even supposing that God did have an emotion of righteous anger and also a desire to act in a certain way, we still fall short of a full explanation as to why God would act in wrath.

We get a bit closer to a fuller explanation (though still not all the way there) if we suppose that an emotion and desire *dispose* God to act in a certain way. Being disposed to act involves a readiness to act: how one would act in a given situation, should that situation arise. Certain biblical references to God's wrath can be read as an indication of God's dispositions. For example, Deuteronomy 29:19-20 warns that those who think, "I will be safe, even though I persist in going my own way," will bring on themselves disaster: "The LORD will never be willing to forgive them; his wrath and zeal will burn against them." This passage can reasonably be read as indicating how God is disposed to act, in cases where a person thinks he is safe but persists in going his own way. Similarly, the stipulation of John 3:36 is that "Whoever believes in the Son has eternal life, but whoever rejects the Son will not see life, for God's wrath remains on them." Again, it is reasonable to read this reference to divine wrath as an indication of how God is disposed to act in cases where a person rejects the Son.

Dispositions, however, are still not actions. Nor are they sufficient to explain an action. It is a person's prerogative, so the saying goes, to change his or her mind. Arguably, the Bible contains references to God changing his mind (for example, Exodus 32:14). I say this is arguable; and indeed theologians and biblical scholars have debated whether such references should be understood as God literally changing his mind and acting in a way different than he had hitherto intended to act. But however the debates about these biblical references should be settled, it remains possible, in principle, for God to change his mind. The alternative would be to suggest that God does not have perfect freedom. That is, the alternative would be to claim that, once God becomes inclined to act in some way, this inclination determines for all eternity that he will act in this way. When the time comes for God to perform the action in question, he is not free to choose *whether* to perform that action. But again this amounts to saying that, in having any disposition, God loses any subsequent freedom to choose when, where, and how to act.[1]

Theologically, this is an absurd conclusion. Surely the only thing that limits God's actions is God's essential nature. It is incoherent to suggest that God might choose to cease to be triune or cease to exist from all eternity. Such scenarios conflict with God's essential attributes of being triune and being eternal. But the characteristic of "always acting in accord with a disposition" is hardly an essential divine attribute.

There is a further reason why a disposition to act in wrath does not explain why God would indeed act in wrath. It is not uncommon to have various dispositions, which sometimes incline one toward conflicting actions. For example, a person may resolve to keep a diet plan that allows for only fruit after supper. If he is then asked at a dinner party whether he would like some chocolate cream pie, he would be disposed to say no, perhaps opting instead for a banana if it's available. But what if he is offered some apple crumble? Well, it contains mostly fruit, to which he is disposed to say yes. But it does contain a moderate amount of sugar and butter, to which his diet resolution disposes him to say no. What will he end up doing? We can only guess.

---

[1]I am sidestepping potential philosophical debates here about God's relationship to time. But for the purposes of this chapter, that debate is not crucial. Even if we suppose that God does not act in time, the point still holds that mere dispositions should not themselves determine God to act in any particular way.

But the point is that there are considerations that would dispose him to act one way *and* another way.

Likewise, a parent may be disposed to react angrily when someone else throws a hard object at her head. The parent may also be disposed to react calmly to her six-month-old child. When the parent one day experiences a whack on the back of her head, she may spin around feeling a rush of anger. But when she sees that her young child has simply been experimenting with throwing his sippy cup for the first time, her disposition to be angry will be moderated by her disposition to react calmly to her six-month-old, who doesn't understand what he's done. Opposing dispositions are not at all uncommon in daily life. In our example, what will the parent's eventual response be? Again we can only guess. (It may depend on what kind of day she is having!) But the point is that having a disposition to act in *one* way does not rule out having another disposition to act a different way.

So let us imagine a case in which God's righteous anger arises. Let us suppose that this angry emotion disposes him to act in some way we would characterize as wrathful. It may well be the case that God has other dispositions that incline him to act in a different way. Indeed, we find in Scripture that righteous anger is only one aspect of God's response to sin. I have named in this chapter some examples of righteous anger in response to sin. But we also find in Scripture the emotional responses of sorrow, grief, loss, disappointment, longing, regret, tenderness, resolve, and so on.

Thus, even if we suppose that God responds to some instance of sin with the emotion of righteous anger, and that this emotion disposes him to act in some way, there are still lots of questions to ask. How does the emotional response of sorrow dispose him to act? What about God's feeling of longing? Or tenderness? Or resolve? In short, the biblical witness specifies righteous anger as one kind of emotional

response God has to sin. There are plenty of other emotional responses we find as well. Perhaps the emotion of anger does dispose
God to act in one particular way. We are still a long way off from
giving a full explanation of God acting in wrath. God will have other
emotions—consistent with the biblical witness—which can dispose
him to act in quite different ways. There is no guarantee that the disposition arising from anger will be the disposition God chooses to
prioritize. I again conclude that a full explanation of God acting in
wrath cannot be found simply in analyzing some single disposition
(or emotion or desire) God has.

THE KEY QUESTION TO ASK ABOUT GOD ACTING IN WRATH

At this point one might ask what *would* amount to a full explanation
of God acting in wrath. If an emotion of righteous anger—even if
coupled with a desire or with a disposition—isn't sufficient to explain
divine acts of wrath, then where is one supposed to look for a sufficient explanation? The answer lies in reflecting on what an intentional
action is.

There are various types of actions people can perform, which we
recognize as part of daily life. On one end of the spectrum, there are
purely reflex actions—as when you close your eye to avoid a bug
flying into it, or when you straighten your leg during a physical exam
after a doctor strikes your knee with a small rubber mallet. At the
other end of the spectrum are genuinely intentional actions, where
you act with the intention of accomplishing some specific goal. Reflective planning is often a part of intentional actions; and when you
act intentionally there is always a reason for acting that can be iden-
tified. (Lying between reflex actions and reflective, intentional actions
are various sorts of other everyday actions: drumming fingers on a
desk while daydreaming, doodling on a piece of paper while listening
to a speech, and so forth.)

God's actions, including acts we associate with wrath, will of course be intentional, or purposeful, actions. As such, they are fully explained only by spelling out the reasons God has in acting—that is, by spelling out the ultimate goal (or goals) God intends to bring about through the action in question. Any analysis of divine wrath will need to identify the reasons, the goals, God has for acting in wrath.

Of course, it is not merely *one* action for which we will be seeking an explanation. The idea of God acting in wrath—which, for example, can fall on the Israelite community (Numbers 1:53), "had broken out against Uzzah" (1 Chronicles 13:11), and was "poured out on Jerusalem" (2 Chronicles 12:7)—typically involves a *pattern* of action. That is, God's wrath involves God's commitment to act in a certain, continued way, again as a means of accomplishing some purpose or goal.

So we arrive at the following question: *What purpose, or goal, is God seeking to achieve when he commits to the pattern of action we associate with God's wrath?* An answer to this question *does* give us an adequate account of divine wrath. That is, it provides a full explanation as to why God would act wrathfully.

I will ultimately be concerned in this book about God's purposes for the *individual*. That is, I will be concerned about what God seeks to achieve in an individual person's life through acts of wrath. Admittedly, the majority of references to God's wrath in Scripture are in the context of God's engagement with nations or groups of people, particularly those in covenant with him. Nevertheless, there is still much in Scripture, particularly in the New Testament, about how an individual can fall under God's wrath. And the biblical descriptions of how God works to shape communities surely have important applications for how God will work to shape the life of an individual. Again, it is my main concern in this book to explore the goals God seeks to achieve in an individual person's life through the pattern of action we associate with God's wrath.

With my characterization of divine wrath as a pattern of action intended to achieve certain *goals*, perhaps one may question whether I have moved too quickly away from the importance of righteous anger as an emotion. One may ask: Even if the emotion of righteous anger isn't the same as an action, isn't God's anger still motivating in some way God's actions when he acts in wrath? After all, many biblical references to divine wrath portray this wrath as being expressed or displayed. For example, Psalm 7:11 speaks of "a God who displays his wrath every day." Couldn't all the passages that reference God's wrath falling on others or being poured out on others naturally be interpreted as God's righteous anger (understood as an emotion) being expressed, or displayed, *through* his pattern of action?

Yet, there are two big problems with trying to explain God's acts of wrath in terms of God being motivated by righteous anger. First, emotions are not necessarily linked with any goal that one believes is a good goal to pursue. That is, they are not necessarily linked with any reason for acting that one believes is a good reason for acting. Consider those times in life where we say that our anger got the better of us. We recognize later on that our actions were not the best actions we could have taken at the time. In such cases, it is not that we made an error of reasoning, reaching the wrong conclusion about the best option to take, all things considered. It is instead that our actions weren't responsive to the reasoning process. The very nature of emotions—whether the emotion of anger or romantic attraction—is that they propel us toward action without us having to make any rational judgments at all.

While humans do sometimes act from our emotions and against our better judgments, such a scenario is inconsistent with an orthodox Christian picture of God. As mentioned earlier, God enjoys perfect freedom. God will never succumb to emotions in acting against his better judgment. Given that God's actions toward us are always intentional actions designed for some purpose, we need to affirm a necessary link between God's acts of wrath and the goals he intends to achieve. We lose this necessary link if we suppose that the final explanation of an act of divine wrath is an emotion like anger.

Second, I have noted that anger is appropriate and indeed good in certain contexts. However, anger is not *always* appropriate. Yes, it is appropriate for a parent to feel protective anger when a toddler runs toward the street. But it is not appropriate for a parent to lash out in anger simply out of embarrassment that other parents are watching. Yes, it is appropriate to be jealous for a spouse's singular, romantic affection. But it is not appropriate to be enraged at a spouse's innocent actions because one is domineering and unduly suspicious.

God's anger is of course always righteous, or appropriate, anger. In specifying *why* God's anger in some instance would be legitimate, rather than illegitimate, we must appeal to the reasons why God is angry. But note what has now happened. The basis for saying God appropriately acts in wrath has to do with considerations other than the emotion itself of anger. The considerations instead have to do with facts about the situation: what it is that is meriting God's disapproval and why God's actions are an appropriate response. We must unpack these details if we want an answer to the question of what is motivating God's appropriate acts in wrath.

All this is not to say that the emotion of anger cannot accompany God's acts of wrath. But there is an important distinction between anger *accompanying* an action and anger *motivating* an action. There would be nothing at all wrong with God's (appropriate) anger accompanying an act we associate with God acting in wrath. But if anger is thought of as the ultimate, motivational ground for an action, then, as a first point, a discussion of reasons and goals becomes irrelevant as a final explanation for the action. And as a second point, we will have lost our ability to say why an act of wrath is appropriate versus inappropriate.

MOVING FORWARD

So we come once again to the question of God's reasons for acting in wrath. Put in the clearest terms: What purposes or goals is God seeking to achieve when he commits to the pattern of action we associate with divine wrath? To begin to answer the question, we need to examine the necessary commitments God already has. That is, we need to examine the patterns of action to which God, by his very nature, is always committed. Whatever purposes God is seeking to achieve through acts of wrath, these purposes must be consistent with his eternal, essential commitments.

2

THE TRINITY AS BENEVOLENT BY NATURE

Any necessary, or essential, commitments God has will stem from his essential nature and attributes. I am using the terms *necessary* and *essential* here in a specific sense. The contrast to *necessary* is *contingent*. There are many contingent facts about God. As Christians we affirm that God created our world, that he became incarnate in the person of Jesus Christ, and that he died on a cross as atonement for the sins of the world. These are core doctrines of the Christian faith.

But they are not *necessary* facts about God. Orthodox Christianity affirms that God did not have to create the world. There is nothing about his nature, his identity, as God that necessitated him creating. Thus, God's standing as Creator is contingent on his free decision to create a world. The same goes for God becoming incarnate in Jesus Christ. God could have chosen to become incarnate at a different time in human history. Jesus' sacrificial death could have occurred in a way that did not involve a cross. If any of these events had changed in its details, God would still be God. His essential nature would not have changed.

On the other hand, there are certain attributes of God, as well as certain actions of God, that are necessary, or essential. If God did not have these attributes, and if God did not perform these actions, then God would not be God. For example, if God did not have the attribute of being eternal, then God would simply not be God. Other essential attributes affirmed by Christians historically include omnipotence, omniscience, perfect freedom, and perfect goodness. If we were talking about someone who didn't possess all these attributes, then assuredly we wouldn't be talking about God. These attributes are essential to God's very nature, to his very identity as God.

THE ESSENTIAL ATTRIBUTE OF LOVE

Another key, essential divine attribute affirmed by Christians is *love*. John makes the well-known—and bold!—claim that "God *is* love" (1 John 4:8). If God's essential nature really is one of love, then his actions will always be consistent with that essential characteristic.

But we will need to pin down what God's love involves exactly. After all, the term *love* is thrown around quite a bit in everyday conversations. People may have very different ideas of exactly what love does and doesn't amount to. The goal moving forward is to identify the commitments God will always have toward us, consistent with his essential attribute of love. The starting point, as we work toward this goal, is to flesh out some of the details of the Christian doctrine of the Trinity.

Orthodox Christian doctrine affirms that God is a tri-personal being: three interdependent persons existing as one substance. This affirmation is not that there are three persons who happen (contingently) to be in relationship. Rather, these relationships are necessary and inseparable. The three persons of the Trinity either exist all together or not at all. Indeed, the names that identify the persons point to this interdependence. The Father can only be a Father if there is a Son; the Spirit is the Spirit of the Father; and so forth.

So Christians will understand the Trinity in terms of persons-in-relationship (again, as opposed to the idea that there are three divine persons who just happen to be in relationship). From eternity, the persons of the Trinity necessarily relate to one another and are dependent on one another for their very existence. It remains a mystery exactly how each of the three persons of the Trinity preserves the existence of the others. Still, this is no more mysterious than the general affirmation that God is a necessary, eternal being. My young nephew once asked during a philosophical discussion, "But *how* is it that God has always existed and doesn't depend on anything outside himself to exist?" There really can be no answer to that question. Such is the nature of a necessary being.

The church has always struggled to capture in language the kind of mutual interdependence that exists among the persons of the Trinity. Jesus claimed that "I am in the Father and the Father is in me" (John 14:11). Paul went so far as to say that "the Lord is the Spirit" (2 Corinthians 3:17), testifying to the sense in which the persons of the Trinity penetrate one another and form one united Godhead—that is, one indissoluble arrangement of interdependent relationships.

At the same time, the three persons of the Trinity remain distinct persons. Jesus, after all, prayed to the Father (Luke 22:42) and spoke of the one (the Holy Spirit) whom the Father would send after him (John 14:26). The persons of the Trinity are united in relationship as one being, or Godhead. What we might call their moral attributes—truthfulness, faithfulness, compassion, and so forth—are also one and the same. In sum, the persons of the Trinity are distinct from one another, though they cannot be separated from one another. (My soul right now is distinct from my body, though it is not separate from my body.)

The church has tried to encapsulate these interdependent relationships within the Trinity with the term *perichoresis*. Steve Seamands provides a good summary of this theological concept.

As the doctrine of the Trinity developed in the church and theologians searched for language to describe the mutual indwelling and interpenetration of the three persons, they eventually landed on the beautiful Greek term *perichoresis*. Perichoresis conveys a number of ideas: reciprocity, interchange, giving to and receiving from one another, being drawn to one another and contained in the other, interpenetrating one another by drawing life from and pouring life into one another as a fellowship of love.[1]

This last line mentions two especially key points as we move to flesh out the implications that the Trinity has for our discussion of God's necessary commitments.

First, there is the key point that the persons of the Trinity give life to one another. This constant purpose of fostering fullness of life in others is a part of God's very nature. Second, there is the explanation that this ongoing act of giving life to others is an ongoing act of love. Once again, in everyday language the term *love* can convey a great variety of meanings. But the specific sense of love eternally on display within the Trinity is most closely associated with the English word *benevolence*: a seeking of others' well-being, a seeking of their fullness of life. Each person of the Trinity pours himself out to the others, for the sake of the others.

This, then, is the necessary commitment the persons of the Trinity have: a continual pattern of pouring oneself out for the good of the other. This ongoing work allows the Trinity to be one being, composed of three interdependent and inseparable persons-in-relationship. Again, my longer-term goal is to identify the commitments toward *us* God will necessarily have, consistent with his essential attributes. But it is crucial to identify God's essential and eternal commitments in order then to explore the implications they have for God's commitments toward us.

Nonessential Attributes of God

Having emphasized the scriptural affirmation that God is love, I should acknowledge that other, similar-sounding affirmations are also

---

[1]Stephen Seamands, *Ministry in the Image of God* (Downers Grove, IL: InterVarsity Press, 2005), 142.

found in Scripture. We read in Scripture that "God is light" (1 John 1:5), that God "is a merciful God" (Deuteronomy 4:31), that God "is a jealous God" (Exodus 34:14), that "God is just" (2 Thessalonians 1:6), and that "God is holy" (Psalm 99:9). Are these also essential attributes of God, just as love is an essential attribute of God? The answer, actually, is no. These attributes are not in the same category as God's attribute of love.

To see the difference between the essential attribute of love and these other attributes, it is helpful to think of the life of God before he created our physical universe. The Christian view of creation is that God did not *have* to create our world or any other world. Nothing necessitated God's creating. Thus, if we want to identify God's essential attributes—the attributes that God could not fail to exhibit and still be God—we must look for those attributes that God has had from all eternity, before the creation of our world.

Is light an essential attribute of God? Well, if it is actual light we're talking about, then the answer is no. Light waves are, after all, a physical part of our universe. That there is any physical light anywhere—emanating from God or from our sun—is contingent on God's free choice to create a physical universe.

Perhaps the references in Scripture to God being light should be interpreted as alluding to God's perfect goodness. Accordingly, the continuation of 1 John 1:5, "in him there is no darkness," could be viewed as a restatement that God has nothing evil or impure in his character. I would certainly affirm that God is light in the metaphorical sense that God's goodness serves as a guiding model for any moral creature that might someday exist. If that is how we should understand the biblical references to God being light, then fair enough. But we cannot interpret them as referring to any essential attribute of (physical) light, on par with the way we affirm God's love as an essential attribute.

God's mercy and God's jealousy are also characteristics of God that are not among his essential ones. God can only extend mercy if there is someone else in the unhappy circumstance of needing forgiveness or relief of some kind. From all eternity, would any of the persons of the Trinity have needed to extend forgiveness or to stoop to offer relief to anyone else within the triune fellowship? Obviously not. So exhibiting mercy cannot be an essential attribute of God. Admittedly, once God *did* create our world, perhaps there is some essential attribute of his that logically implies that he will (necessarily) act mercifully in some context. That would be a larger discussion, and we would have to begin by identifying that essential attribute (love?) and showing why mercy necessarily derives from it. But the point here is that mercy itself is not one of God's essential attributes.

A similar discussion can be applied to God's jealousy. Jealousy has no place within the eternal fellowship among Father, Son, and Holy Spirit. There is no action that could possibly be committed by any person of the Trinity that would fall short of others' legitimate expectation, leading to legitimate feelings of jealousy. The impossibility of jealousy ever arising stems from other essential attributes that God has: his perfect love and goodness (which translate to acting always in ways that meet legitimate expectations) and his omniscience (knowing what these legitimate expectations are). In short, however we interpret passages that state that God is a jealous God, these references cannot be to one of God's essential attributes.

Is God's Justice an Essential Attribute?

Whether justice is an essential attribute may be a trickier question, largely because there are quite a variety of meanings historically that have been given to that term. So-called procedural justice involves fair processes for ruling on disputes between individuals and for assessing accusations against an individual. Deuteronomy 1:16-17 speaks to this kind of justice: "Hear the disputes between your people and judge fairly, whether the case is between two Israelites or between an Israelite and a foreigner residing among you. Do not show partiality in judging; hear both small and great alike." Commutative justice involves fairness in the exchange of goods and services. Biblical passages speak to this kind of justice: "Differing weights and differing measures—the LORD detests them both" (Proverbs 20:10).

In addition to these two types of justice, the political and legal systems of modern Western societies focus heavily on distributive justice and on retributive justice. Distributive justice involves the fair allocation of a society's (inevitably limited) resources. Retributive justice involves the fair punishment that victims can rightly expect to be exacted on those who have wronged them.

Debates in modern times about these last two types of justice are well rehearsed. We debate questions of distributive justice when we ask about a just tax system. The biblical references to justice sometimes include the concern of distributive justice. For instance, we read in Deuteronomy 10:18-19 that the Lord "defends the cause of the fatherless and the widow, and loves the foreigner residing among you, giving them food and clothing. And you are to love those who are foreigners, for you yourselves were foreigners in Egypt."

Modern debates about retributive justice are also easy to recognize. For instance, what is an appropriate punishment for financial fraud? Should prison sentences for violent crimes always be longer than for financial fraud and other nonviolent crimes? Questions of retributive justice are addressed in various passages in Scripture: "Eye for eye, tooth for tooth" (Exodus 21:24); "Whoever sheds human blood, by humans shall their blood be shed" (Genesis 9:6); and "God is just: He will pay back trouble to those who trouble you" (2 Thessalonians 1:6).

None of the types of justice discussed thus far seem to be good candidates for inclusion among God's essential attributes. Again, it's

helpful to think of God's life before he created the universe. Procedural justice would not be operative within the Trinity from eternity;
its need only arises when there are disputes or accusations to process.
Likewise, because the Father, Son, and Holy Spirit could never wrong
one another, retributive justice would never be operative. Questions
of commutative and distributive justice are perhaps not as immediately clear. Perhaps one might suggest that the exchanges of fellowship
among the persons of the Trinity are always fair and just, along with
the distribution of each person's self-giving. But in truth, distributive
justice is only operative on the assumption that resources are limited
(and that all parties cannot have their unlimited fill). Commutative
justice assumes a transactional model of commodity exchange, which
does not at all capture the self-giving outpouring within the theological model of *perichoresis*.

One last type of justice might conceivably be a candidate for an
essential attribute of God. Some Christian writers speak of justice
within the Bible in terms of "restoration to community."[2] So-called
restorative justice will involve the restoration of socioeconomic
wholeness, so that one can participate fully within a community.
Plenty of passages in Scripture do indeed focus on this idea of restoration. For example, we read God's instruction to the Israelite people:
"When you reap the harvest of your land, do not reap to the very edges
of your field or gather the gleanings of your harvest. Do not go over
your vineyard a second time or pick up the grapes that have fallen.
Leave them for the poor and the foreigner" (Leviticus 19:9-10). The
instruction of Leviticus 25:25-28 is that, if other Israelites need to sell
their property and do not in the following years acquire the money to
redeem it, "it will be returned in the Jubilee, and they can then go back
to their property." Thus after fifty years ownership reverts to the

---

[2]Stephen Mott and Ronald Sider, "Economic Justice: A Biblical Paradigm," in *Toward a Just and
Caring Society*, ed. David Gushee (Grand Rapids: Baker Books, 1999), 31.

original family, so as to avoid an increasing cycle of poverty. Restoration in these instances seems to supersede concerns of commutative and procedural justice, which would otherwise entitle the owner to use his property as he freely chooses.

But does the idea of restoration fall under the category of justice? It seems fair to say that the ultimate goal of God's instructions about such matters as procedural justice (not showing favoritism) and commutative justice (using consistent weights and measures in business) is full participation and flourishing for everyone in the community. It is also true that God's essential nature includes this attribute of furthering fullness of life for others. As we have seen, the idea of *perichoresis* among the persons of the Trinity involves the commitment to offer life to one another, enabling participation within the triune community.

But, again, is this a matter of justice? The Bible's use of that term is at times very wide. For instance, the NRSV uses that term in describing God as one "who executes justice for the orphan and the widow, and who loves the strangers, providing them food and clothing" (Deuteronomy 10:18). Here the terms *justice* and *love* seem to be used interchangeably. In Job's cry for a just verdict on his life, he seemingly includes as matters of justice providing food and water for the hungry, the widowed, and the fatherless (Job 22:7; 31:16-17). Stephen Mott and Ronald Sider conclude that the goal of biblical justice is "not primarily the recovery of the integrity of the legal system. It is the restoration of the community as a place where all live together in wholeness."[3] The significance of God's concern in Scripture for the poor and marginalized perhaps explains why our care for them is described in terms of justice. That term reinforces the nonnegotiable aspect of God's instructions to us to care for those on the margins. But the question I

---

[3]Mott and Sider, "Economic Justice," 33.

have been considering is whether themes of restoration really are properly called matters of justice.

Some Eastern societies today might perhaps view these themes as matters of justice. This is because these Eastern societies can operate with a rather expanded concept of justice. For instance, stories are well-known in which a judge's decision in a court case may hinge significantly on whether the accused has helped restore the victim of his crime in some way, including financially. A judge may hand down a much lighter sentence if there is evidence that the victim has been compensated in some way.

But this concept of justice is quite far removed from the much narrower framework of justice that operates within modern Western societies. If we were to learn that a person on criminal trial tried to pay off the victim as a way of mitigating a possible prison sentence, we would regard this as an attempt to *subvert* justice. Thinking back to those passages from Leviticus and Deuteronomy about forgiving debt and allowing the poor to glean one's fields, concern for the poor would never trump property rights as a matter of *justice* (as that term is conceived in modern Western societies). Yes, we might out of compassion want to pass laws that provide resources for the poor that go beyond what procedural, commutative, and distributive justice require. But this would reflect our view that our concern for the restoration of the poor should trump our concern that strict justice should always be administered.

To sum up, if we stick to an understanding of justice familiar to those of us in Western societies, then so-called restorative justice really doesn't fall under the category of justice. I acknowledge that God's essential nature includes bringing fullness of life to others. If someone wants to *call* this restorative justice, then I would agree that this kind of justice is essential to God's nature.[4] But sticking to the way

---

[4]The implication here wouldn't be that the three persons of the Trinity eternally need *restoring*. Rather, the idea would be that what we call restorative justice is nothing more than God

that justice is typically understood in modern, Western societies—as procedural, commutative, distributive, and retributive—God's *essential* nature would not be one of justice, though of course God will always act justly in a world where there are shortages and brokenness. To put the point another way, in explaining why God will always act justly in our world, we would have to appeal to some other attribute of God that *is* essential to God's nature and from which God's justice is derived.

Is Holiness an Essential Attribute?

A final attribute I want to consider is God's holiness. The term *holiness* is often used quite broadly in Christian circles. Leading a holy life can be associated with living a pure life, a morally upright life, a godly life. We might hear a church referred to as a holy place, with this reference indicating that one should be reverent when inside that church. We might hear an elderly saint within the church referred to as having grown in holiness during her life, signifying that she has grown in spiritual maturity over the years.

In truth, the early references we find in Scripture to God's holiness are not so much references to any moral quality in God. Rather, holiness was a way of describing the uniqueness or otherness of God. In its original use, to emphasize that God is holy is to emphasize that God is other than we are. Strictly speaking, the concept alone of holiness does not yet tell us what this other, uniquely different God is like.

Moving beyond God's revelation that he is holy, in Scripture we find that God does go on to reveal to his people the moral qualities he has. In Leviticus 19:2 God instructs Moses to tell the entire assembly of Israel: "Be holy because I, the LORD your God, am holy." We then immediately find out what is involved in reflecting God's character

---

simply bringing fullness of life to others, which manifests itself in restoration where others may lack something.

and priorities. The people are to make provisions for the poor and for foreigners (Leviticus 19:9). They are not to deceive one another (Leviticus 19:11). They are not to defraud one another or hold back the wages of hired workers (Leviticus 19:13). As a general principle, each person is to "love your neighbor as yourself" (Leviticus 19:18).

Of course, even as we humans try to reflect God's character and priorities in these ways, we inevitably fall short of fully mirroring God. God's holiness, or otherness, expresses the way that there is in God an absolute integrity and purity of motives. While we seek to reflect these traits, we will inevitably do so imperfectly.

This chasm between God and us led Isaiah to despair. God's holiness was key for Isaiah in shaping his own understanding of God as well as in his calling to be a prophet. His commissioning begins with hearing the angelic chorus: "Holy, holy, holy is the LORD Almighty; the whole earth is full of his glory" (Isaiah 6:3). But this immediately raises a crisis for Isaiah. "I am ruined! For I am a man of unclean lips, and I live among a people of unclean lips, and my eyes have seen the King, the LORD Almighty" (Isaiah 6:5). In Isaiah and throughout much of the Old Testament, references to God's holiness are intended to emphasize God's purity, his righteousness, his absolute separateness from sin or immorality.

So what should we conclude on the question of whether holiness is part of God's essential nature? If we stick with the original meaning of holiness as "other," then indeed God is essentially a unique being, distinct from any other being that does or might exist. Affirming that God is holy is very much like affirming that God exists necessarily, that God is self-sustaining, and that God transcends everything else that could ever exist. If we go on to connect the idea of holiness specifically to God's separateness from sin, then this attribute would not be an essential attribute in a strict sense. Rather, in this context God's "holiness" would be a relational attribute. That is, it would describe God's relationship to sin: specifically, that he is separate from it. Since sin does not eternally exist, God's relationship to sin could obviously not be an essential attribute. (And of course any subsequent response of God to sin—such as wrath—could also not be an essential attribute.)

The discussion of holiness in this section, as well as the discussion of justice from the previous section, lays the groundwork for the analysis I will offer later on in chapter four. In this present chapter, the takeaway points from our discussion about justice and holiness are as follows.

God's attribute of justice is not essential to God's nature in the way that his attribute of love is essential. God's justice is only needed in a world (such as ours) where there are imperfections and shortages. God essential nature is therefore not just. As regards God's holiness, God is essentially holy. Yet, affirming that God is holy does not yet settle the question of what God's moral characteristics, priorities, and commitments are. Christians go on of course to describe God as pure, righteous, morally good. Having noted the purity of God, we might then use the term *holiness* to refer to God's separateness from sin. However, on this understanding of holiness, the term would not describe God's essential nature, but rather his relationship to the contingent sin in our world.

POSITIONING LOVE AND WRATH AS DIVINE ATTRIBUTES

It should be quite obvious from the discussion of God's love, justice, and holiness that God's wrath could not possibly be an essential divine attribute. God would not from eternity be displaying wrath, even before sin and evil entered the world. Whatever the relationship between God's love and God's wrath turns out to be, comparing the two is therefore in a sense like comparing apples to oranges. Yes, Paul tells us to consider both the "kindness and sternness of God"

(Romans 11:22). The King James Version of the Bible puts it in terms of the "goodness and severity of God." Nevertheless, the goodness and love of God are necessary characteristics God will *always* have, no matter the circumstance. Conversely, God's response of sternness or severity or wrath will always be conditional and subject to change. Biblical scholar John Goldingay puts it like this: "Anger is not a divine attribute in the same sense as love is; the instinct to love emerges from God without any outside stimulus, but God gets angry only as a re-action to outside stimulus."[5]

This point does not by itself settle the issue of whether God's response to a person in some given circumstance will be more closely associated with love or with wrath. But for now it is worth noting the variety of ways in Scripture in which we find the enduring quality of God's love emphasized, in contrast to the provisional nature of God's wrath. We might say that there is an overriding bias in God toward love and not toward wrath.

God's love certainly precedes wrath in the biblical narrative. God's love precedes not only any breaking of the Mosaic law; it precedes the very giving of the law. God acts to deliver his people from Egypt and then sets out the standards by which his people are to live if they are to stay in healthy relationship with him and with one another. God has of course already made an "everlasting covenant" with Abraham and his descendants (Genesis 17:7). Much later in the Old Testament, when his people have repeatedly broken their covenant with God, God's promise is still to "remember the covenant I made with you"—and then to "establish an everlasting covenant with you" (Ezekiel 16:60).

The permanence of this covenant, established in God's love for his people, is contrasted with the limits God places on his wrath. God's

---

[5]John Goldingay, *Old Testament Theology*, vol. 2, *Israel's Faith* (Downers Grove, IL: IVP Academic, 2006), 141.

anger toward his people is repeatedly described as being constrained or curtailed in some way. The psalmist notes how, when people "were not loyal to him" and "were not faithful to his covenant," nevertheless "time after time he restrained his anger and did not stir up his full wrath" (Psalm 78:37-38). At times we find an individual petitioning God to turn from his anger, reminding God of the permanence of his loving covenant toward his people. For instance, Moses implores God to limit his anger against the Israelite people when they cast an idol in the shape of a calf. Consequently, "the LORD relented and did not bring on his people the disaster he had threatened" (Exodus 32:14). Amos offers a similar petition (Amos 7:1-6), and Abraham appeals to God's bias for love over wrath in interceding on behalf of Sodom (Genesis 18:20-33).

Moses himself finds he must again petition God to turn from his anger against the Israelite people, this time at the height of their grumbling about their living conditions (Numbers 14:11-19). What's particularly interesting is that Moses repeats to God the very words God had earlier used to describe himself: "The LORD is slow to anger, abounding in love and forgiving sin and rebellion" (Numbers 14:18). The fuller passage comes from Exodus 34:6-7, when God proclaimed his name to Moses on Mount Sinai: "The LORD, the LORD, the compassionate and gracious God, slow to anger, abounding in love and faithfulness, maintaining love to thousands, and forgiving wickedness, rebellion and sin. Yet he does not leave the guilty unpunished; he punishes the children and their children for the sin of the parents to the third and fourth generation."

Since it was common in ancient Israel for multiple generations to live under the same roof, the reference to God punishing "to the third and fourth generation" may be a way of talking of how God's discipline inevitably impacts an entire family. But even if we do interpret this passage as God extending punishment over time to several generations, the crucial contrast in the passage is that God maintains love to the *thousandth* generation. The sentence structure of this passage makes this point clear enough. Indeed Moses explicitly makes the point in Deuteronomy 7:9: "He is the faithful God, keeping his covenant of love to a thousand generations of those who love him and keep his commandments." Again, the permanence of God's love is contrasted with the more provisional nature of God's wrath.

While God's love flows from his very nature, I will argue in later chapters that wrath is best viewed as one strategy God has to restore people to a relationship of love with himself. Even so, such a strategy will always seem in a sense out of place. Isaiah's message of God's judgment, a message that will bring "sheer terror" (Isaiah 28:19), is described as God's "strange" work. Isaiah declares: "The LORD will rise up as he did at Mount Perazim, he will rouse himself as in the Valley of Gibeon—to do his work, his strange work, and perform his task, his alien task" (Isaiah 28:21). God's harsh judgments are "strange" and "alien" to the people precisely because the dominant framework for seeing God is one in which God is slow to anger, abounding in love.

As regards God's love and God's wrath, the biblical narrative makes it clear in a variety of ways that God's love is essential to God's character in a way that God's wrath is not. There exists some kind of important asymmetry between God's love and God's wrath. As God relates to us, there is a kind of permanence, or priority, or bias toward love. Whatever the specific ways in which God's wrath relates to his love, the uniquely central place of God's love will have to be preserved.

MOVING FORWARD

Let us take stock of our discussions to this point. I noted in chapter one that God's wrath involves a commitment to a pattern of action that purposefully affects others for some intended goal. Whatever these goals are, they must be consistent with any essential commitments of God. So our search in this chapter has been for God's essential commitments.

The key essential attribute of God that *does* involve a pattern of action is God's attribute of love. Love here is understood along the lines of benevolence: a giving of oneself to others so as to provide them fullness of life. The benevolent patterns of action represented by the affirmation "God is love" are the very actions that bind the persons of the Trinity together. These actions of love are part of the explanation as to why God is self-sustaining and exists necessarily.

We have looked in this chapter at other potential candidates for essential divine attributes that would necessitate divine commitments. Justice ends up not being an essential attribute of God. Holiness, while essential to God's nature, does not by itself shed light on what God's commitments might be.

Here is why all this is so important for our discussion about divine wrath. In later chapters I will explore the goals God could be committed to pursuing when he acts in wrath. Whatever these commitments are, they must be consistent with the essential, trinitarian commitments to bring fullness of life to others through the giving of oneself. That is, God's commitments must be consistent with his love. A next step will be to look at what God's essential love implies about how he will act toward *us*.

3

DOES LOVE ALWAYS SEEK
OUR FLOURISHING?

In the previous chapter we saw how an orthodox Christian doctrine of God implies that the persons of the Trinity have essential commitments to bring fullness of life to one another. But does God also have a corresponding, necessary commitment always to seek the flourishing of all *humans*?

THE INVITATION TO LIFE WITHIN THE TRINITY

The Christian Scriptures emphasize the unique role of humans within the created order. Humans alone are said to be created in God's image, and they have the capacity to engage in a particular kind of relationship with God. Indeed, a continual theme in the biblical narrative is that God invites us into an interpersonal relationship, drawing and enabling us to say yes to this invitation.

This invitation is nothing less than the invitation to participation within the very life of God. Trinitarian doctrine affirms that the Holy Spirit draws, or prompts, us so that we might move toward this relationship. The Holy Spirit prompts us to join Christ in offering prayers, works of service, and other acts of commitment. These positive responses to God's prompting grace are offered with Christ *to* the Father. (Thus the orthodox Christian statement that we offer our lives *to* the Father, *through* and *with* the Son, and *in* the power of the Holy Spirit.) Centrally, one thing we offer with Christ to the Father is Christ's perfect sacrifice on the cross. We are able to offer Christ's sacrifice as atonement for our own sins when we make Christ the Lord of our lives, folding our lives into his larger life story and availing ourselves of the merits he makes available to us as the one who now takes responsibility for us as our Lord.

The point I want to emphasize is that humans are invited in a very real sense to participate in the life of God. The Father sends the Holy Spirit to prompt us. We respond by joining Christ in the work he has already initiated in his ministry of reconciling the world to God. This work is our offering of love to the Father and is offered with Christ, who also asks the Father to send again the Holy Spirit. So the cycle continues. We come to participate in the enduring fellowship among the persons of the Trinity.

Even so, does the commitment of benevolence that the persons of the Trinity have to one another extend to all humans who are invited to participate in fellowship with God? Jesus' recorded statements in the Gospel of John link the love within the Trinity to God's love for us. Consider John 15:9: "As the Father has loved me, so have I loved you." Still, while there may be some key points at which the love within the Trinity is extended to humans, there are obviously some enormous differences between humans and any person of the Trinity. There is no question, for instance, of the Father relating to anyone but the eternal Son as the one who reconciles the world to God. The Father loves the Son *as* the one who redeems the world. Obviously, the Father does not love humans in that way.

The crucial question for our purposes is this: Do the persons of the Trinity necessarily relate to humans with unwavering benevolence—that is, with a continued pursuit of all humans' well-being? God has revealed to us in Scripture that he loves us. But how do we determine whether this revelation implies that God is committed to benevolent patterns of action toward all people at all times? Another way of asking this question is to ask how far the analogy of John 15:9 extends (between the Father's love for Christ and Christ's love for us) on the specific point of a commitment to benevolent patterns of action.

THE ANALOGY WITHIN GOD'S CLAIM THAT HE LOVES US

Thomas Aquinas (1225–1274) highlighted the advantages of using analogy in our descriptions of God's attributes. Analogical language avoids the twin errors, Aquinas emphasized, of univocal and equivocal language in our descriptions. If a person uses the same term to describe two different things, and if she uses that term univocally, that means she is applying the term equally in both cases. For example, when she comments that the soup was *hot* and burned her tongue, and that the coffee was *hot* and burned her tongue, she is using the term *hot* in the same exact sense. She is referring to a high temperature. On the other hand, if she uses a term equivocally, that means she is using the term to mean *one* thing in the first case but using the term to mean something entirely different in the other case. For example, when she then says that her friend Jerry bought a *hot* little sports car, she is using this term in a completely different sense from the sense of *hot* used when describing the soup.

Somewhere between univocal language and equivocal language lies analogical language. If the person comments that the chicken vindaloo was way too *hot*, she is using that term in a sense that is analogous to the sense in which the soup was hot. It is not that the chicken vindaloo had too high a temperature, so the sense of *hot* is not univocal. But neither is the sense equivocal. The burning of her tongue from the spicy chicken feels similar to the burning from the hot soup, and in each case her reflex action is to reach for a glass of water. These similarities show that the sense in which the chicken vindaloo is *hot* is analogous to the sense in which the soup is *hot*.

Aquinas's insight was that our language about God will inevitably be analogous. There will always be some differences between human attributes and divine attributes. But there will nevertheless be similarities if our claims about God are to have any meaning. If someone were to suggest that God's love is *wholly* different from human love, then, for all we know, divine love might most closely resemble human capriciousness or human gloominess. The similarities between human love and divine love must ground our understanding of divine love, if the affirmation that God is love is to have any meaning for us. This is so even with the acknowledgment, following Aquinas, that we will never fully understand the ways in which divine love is different from human love.

God again reveals to us that he loves us. A revelation, by definition, implies that the recipients of a message have understood its essential content. (Otherwise, the attempted revelation wouldn't have been a successful one!) In order for us to understand God's revelation that he loves us, God must rely on similarities between divine love and human love. That is, God must rely on our use of analogy. He must rely on our ability to connect his revelation (that he loves us) to our prior understanding of what the concept of love involves. The reason for this process does not stem from anything unique about receiving communication from God. Rather, the reason simply has to do with the way we humans learn the meaning of love or any such concept within a language.

How We Come to Understand the Concept of Love

My fifth-grade teacher was a wonderful woman and educator. But I wish I could go back to fifth grade and contest one particular point she routinely made to the class. When the class would come to a key term in our studies, she would ask whether anyone could define the term. For example, in a social-studies lesson on equality and discrimination,

I remember her asking whether anyone could define *prejudice*. We students would raise our hands and say, "Well, it's like when someone has followed all the rules, but you still penalize them." "Or when two people are equally qualified for some job, but you give the job to one person just because of his race." Our teacher would then respond, "No, those are *examples*. I'm asking for a *definition*." It seemed like we children were forever falling into that error of confusing an example with a definition—or so our teacher would repeatedly tell us!

But the truth is, for many concepts, examples are precisely the way we learn their meaning. Indeed, examples are the only way we learn their meaning. To put the point another way, examples are what give these concepts their content. Here's an explanation of what I mean.

Consider how a person from early childhood begins to learn about the concept of kindness. While a toddler, the child might throw food at her older brother during a family meal. Her parents will chasten her: "Now, Anna, that's not kind. You must say, 'Sorry.'" She may say "sorry" and then add "I love you" to her brother. Her parents will smile and say, "Oh, Anna, now that is a kind thing to say!" Later on, while attending a play group, another child may snatch one of Anna's toys. Anna runs to her parents in tears and tells the story. "Well, that wasn't a very kind thing to do, was it?" they will say, before devising a strategy to address the matter. On the other hand, if another child volunteers to share his favorite toy with Anna, they will say, "That was very kind of him, wasn't it? Shall we say 'Thank you' to him?"

And so the lessons go on, building on repeated examples as Anna grows to have a firmer and firmer grasp of the concept of kindness. Her firmness of grasp is due to the widening pool of examples that give content to the concept of kindness. As yet, we imagine that Anna could not distinguish among the concepts of politeness, charity, and generosity. These concepts are certainly not identical. Some actions are charitable but not generous (such as giving ten cents to World

Vision). Some actions are generous but not polite (such as tossing a hundred-dollar bill to a neighbor and gruffly saying, "Here, take it"). Some actions are polite but not charitable (such as turning down a request for a donation with tactful words and a warm smile).

But at present, young Anna cannot appreciate the more subtle differences among these concepts. In her mind, we imagine that they would all qualify simply as kind. After all, she as yet only has a small pool of examples that give content to her concept of kindness. As she grows older and is exposed to more and more examples, she will be able to see patterns among those actions that her parents term charitable but not generous. That is, she will have a growing understanding of the kinds of actions that would count as charitable but not generous (and would count as generous but not polite, and so forth). In short, Anna will become able to distinguish among more and more concepts. Again, it is the real-life examples to which she relates the various concepts she is learning that give these various concepts their content.

Circling back to my fifth-grade classroom, here is the problem with the teacher's sharp distinction between definitions and examples. Definitions themselves often provide no real content to concepts such as kindness. Definitions typically rely on synonyms. So, for example, my Oxford English Dictionary informs me that kindness means "being friendly, generous, and considerate." But ultimately there's a problem if we simply use terms to define other terms. We end up saying that kindness means to be friendly and generous. What does *friendly* mean? Well, it means to be generous and kind. And of course to be generous is to be friendly and kind.

The problem of circularity should be pretty obvious. The only way these concepts gain any real content is if we relate them to examples. Just like Anna from our previous discussion, we need to be able to draw on a pool of real-life examples that count as instances of kindness.

This is what allows us to assign terms such as *kindness* a definite meaning. Further, there is again the problem that concepts such as kindness, friendliness, charitableness, and generosity do not mean *exactly* the same thing. Their differences can only be grasped by distinguishing the pools of examples that do and do not merit the descriptions of these respective terms.

If we are to communicate with one another using terms such as *kindness* or *charitableness*, we must have broad agreement about the kinds of examples that would count as kind and as charitable. Such is the nature of public language. Interestingly, the meaning of conceptual terms can and often does change over time. For instance, the English word *believe* used to mean "to cherish, to cling to." If I had "belief" toward someone, that would mean that I had affection of some kind toward the person. Today, *believe* means "to assent to, to think to be true." I can have beliefs about some person while thinking the person a perfect scoundrel. Why terms change their meaning over time is an interesting question, with probably a variety of answers. *How* a term changes its meaning is straightforward: the public consensus changes as to which kinds of examples would count as an instance of *belief* (or as an instance of whatever other conceptual term we are investigating).

The key takeaway point remains that, in order for us to communicate with one another using conceptual terms within a given public language, we must have a broad agreement about the examples that give content to those terms. The importance of this point becomes clear as we return to Aquinas's discussion of analogical language and connect it to the question of whether God's love entails a benevolent commitment toward us at all times.

THE PREVAILING MODEL THAT GOD IS LOVE

The Bible contains a number of different models for how we should understand God's relationship with us and his commitment to us:

king, shepherd, high priest, rock, and so forth. The prevailing model within God's self-revelation, however, is God as father. Jesus' recorded prayers are directed to his Father (John 17:1). Jesus' encouragement is that his followers should relate to God as their heavenly Father: "This, then, is how you should pray: 'Our Father in heaven . . .'" (Matthew 6:9). Consistent with the divine attribute of love, our chief, enduring model of God becomes that of loving father.

This particular model will not of course be a perfect one. God's attributes and commitments will not correspond in every way with a loving human father. Still, following Aquinas, we gain understanding of God from this revealed analogy only on the assumption that there are some key similarities between the pattern of actions indicative of a loving human father and the pattern of actions of God as our loving heavenly Father. Moreover, we should expect these similarities to be especially significant, given that the model of a loving father is again the prevailing model in Scripture and thus the one we should presume to be most analogous to the ways in which God acts toward us.

Consider now the role that continued benevolence plays in our descriptions of a loving earthly father. Our individual concepts will likely vary at particular points as to what an ideally loving earthly father would look like. But surely we will all agree that an earthly father would not merit the description *loving* if he ceased at any point to have his child's long-term well-being as an ultimate goal. Surely we will agree that this goal must be one he maintains for each of his children. This ultimate goal is simply not negotiable, given the role of responsibility we all recognize parents as having for their children.

By saying this commitment is not negotiable, I am referring back to our earlier discussion of how terms such as *loving* take on meaning for us. If we think back to the example of the child named Anna, we might suppose that she witnesses a scene in which one child bites another child. Suppose someone then said, "That was a kind thing to do, wasn't it?" Anna would be confused by the question. Her answer would be, "No, that's not kind!" The reason for her answer is this: the example stands in too stark a contrast with the examples by which she learned the term *kind*. If this new action were also to count as kind, then the term has simply lost any identifiable content for her. In such a case, a description of *kind* would no longer communicate anything substantive to her. She would not know what the attribute kindness referred to. Thus the example of biting is not negotiable as an example of kindness; it is ruled out if the term is to retain any meaning. For corresponding reasons, it seems obvious that our shared, general understanding of a loving father stands too starkly at odds with an example of a father who fails to be committed to his child's long-term well-being. If a father's failure to pursue his child's flourishing were to count as an instance of loving, then that term would no longer convey any meaning to us.

To be sure, there are borderline cases about what might count as loving. We might debate, for instance, whether a particular act of tough love really was entirely loving or whether it partially lapsed into resentment or cruelty. But the failure to be committed to a child's flourishing as an ultimate goal is just not negotiable. Such a failure surely is far outside the kinds of examples through which we have a shared, general idea of the commitments any earthly father must have in order to qualify as loving.

Admittedly, in a number of contexts Christians are right to point to God's affirmation that "As the heavens are higher than the earth, so are my ways higher than your ways and my thoughts than your thoughts" (Isaiah 55:9). Within the context of God's benevolent commitments to us, it oftentimes may be a mystery *how* God is seeking our long-term well-being. Probably we will always have in this life only a very partial grasp of how God is using the events around us to shape us and others into the likeness of Christ. But it cannot be a mystery to us whether God remains committed to our ultimate flourishing. At least, this cannot be a mystery given the core Christian affirmation that God loves us as our heavenly Father.

It is certainly true that God's revelation in Jesus Christ expands our understanding of what genuine love entails. The incarnation shows us how love may involve stooping in humility to meet others where they are. Christ's death on the cross reinforces his astonishing teaching that love may need to be extended to those who have their backs to us, even to those who have made us their enemies. Such was the love of Christ for us, as well as the love for us of the Father, who had to watch the agonizing mistreatment of his beloved Son. The shared love the Son and the Father have for us led them to absorb great costs in doing the most that could be done to draw us into the life of the Trinity.

Such examples give us a deeper understanding of what an ideal loving father (or an ideal loving friend) can look like. That is, the examples expand—in sometimes very unanticipated ways—the pool of examples that give content to our concept of a loving father. Yet, the point remains that these examples are not in stark contrast to the best examples we already had of a loving earthly father. If they *were* in sharp contrast, then the revealed analogy that God is our loving Father in heaven would be no revelation to us at all, for the meaning of loving father would be lost on us. We would no longer have any general understanding of what that affirmation implied, since we would be baffled as to what kinds of examples represented the commitments of a loving father.

DOES THE GOD OF THE BIBLE
REALLY SEEK ALL PEOPLE'S WELL-BEING?

So far in this chapter I have been fleshing out some of the implications of the core Christian affirmation that God is love. I started with God's revelation to us that he loves us as a loving father loves us. I have shown why this revelation can only have meaning to us humans if there are some important similarities between God's love and the best examples of a human father's love for his children.

This line of argument simply uses the tools of philosophical reasoning to flesh out the implications that God is love and that he loves us in a way that bears some recognizable analogy to the love of a human father. But whatever the merits of this more philosophical line of argument, one might question whether the Bible allows us to conclude that God really does seek the well-being of *all* people. Throughout Scripture there are references to God's "chosen people" and to those who "belong to him." They play a special role as God's children. But what of those people who do *not* belong to him? Doesn't Scripture suggest—or perhaps even plainly state!—that God is not committed to their well-being in the same way?

To survey the entire biblical narrative would be far too big a topic to include in this book. But I want to look at two specific examples from Scripture. In my experience, these are the two examples most commonly cited in support of the claim that God isn't equally committed to the well-being of all people. By tackling these two examples, I hope to give a response that could then be used in helping address other examples that might potentially be raised from Scripture.

One crucial distinction is important to emphasize before I look at the two examples: the distinction is between an ultimate goal and an intermediate goal. A person's ultimate goal may be to remain healthy into old age. As a means of achieving this goal, the person may try to get his heart rate up for twenty minutes each day and to eat five servings of vegetables each day. These are intermediate goals. That is, they are goals he sets as a means of achieving his ultimate goal of staying healthy. By themselves, the daily goals of sustained exercise and eating healthy may at times be unattractive. On certain days he may loathe getting on the treadmill or forgoing the donut in favor of another kale smoothie. But he commits to these intermediate goals because of his ultimate goal of remaining healthy into old age.

Now, on the matter of whether God seeks all people's well-being, we can distinguish two questions. First, there is the question of whether God always retains as an *ultimate* goal all people's long-term well-being. Second, there is the question of whether God always has as an intermediate goal all people's more immediate well-being. A parent who disciplines a child compromises her child's more immediate happiness (by grounding the child, taking away some privilege, etc.). But the parent may do this because of the ultimate goal of ensuring that the child develops the kind of moral character needed for a deeper kind of long-term flourishing. In later chapters I will show how God's wrath can be viewed as a particular type of discipline for the ultimate purpose of drawing people into relationship with him. But in this section I am merely looking at the question of whether Scripture is consistent with the philosophical argument that God seeks all people's flourishing as an ultimate goal.

I mentioned that two examples from Scripture seem to be most cited by those who contend that God does not necessarily seek all people's flourishing as an ultimate goal. The first example involves the conquest narrative in the Old Testament, which depicts God guiding his chosen people into the promised land of Canaan. By favoring Israel as his special or chosen race of people, does God treat the Canaanites as dispensable?

Richard Dawkins is one who finds the Old Testament's conquest narrative to be morally reprehensible. He describes it as an "ethnic cleansing" brazenly depicted in the book of Joshua with "xenophobic relish."[1] Notwithstanding the rhetorical flourish in this comment, is there nonetheless a genuine problem raised? After all, we condemn

---

[1]Richard Dawkins, *The God Delusion* (London: Bantam, 2007), 280.

Hitler for policies of extermination and seizure of others' property. Isn't the conquest narrative at least a comparable policy? Even if there are differences, at the very least doesn't the conquest narrative show that God is significantly *less* concerned with the well-being of the Canaanites than with the Israelite people?

I'm convinced that the answer to both questions is no. Reading about any group of people being displaced from their land is always disturbing. A basic sensitivity to human distress should cause us all to identify at some level with the plight of Canaanite families being displaced. At the same time, the conquest narrative is not comparable to the actions of a dictator who dispossesses people of the homes they rightfully own.

When we hear the conquest narrative through modern ears, we cannot help but assume a framework of property rights. We assume that whoever lives in a place may rightfully claim to own it, unless there is reason to think they have taken possession of the property dishonestly. But the Bible never thinks in these terms. The idea of property rights, as well as the idea of a sovereign nation-state, is a relatively modern idea. Within the Bible the whole world and all its people belong to God (Psalm 24:1). From this viewpoint no single person has an inalienable right to a piece of land. People always hold the land as tenants responsible to God. Hence, Israel could lose the land if it was unfaithful to God (Leviticus 26:27-33; Deuteronomy 28:64-68).

Because the land belonged to God, he could give it to Israel. The land was initially promised to Abraham (Genesis 12:7; 15:7-21), and entry into it was always the goal of the exodus. But there was a delay between promise and entry into the land. Interestingly, the conquest narrative gives a reason for this delay: "for the sin of the Amorites has not yet reached its full measure" (Genesis 15:16). (The Amorites here represent the broader population within Canaan.) Israel only received the land when the Canaanites had thoroughly and decisively rejected God's purposes.

It is not simply that God favors Israel above others. Rather, in establishing Israel as the people through whom his purposes will be carried out, a land is needed. The land God gives is one where the local population stand under judgment. Again, the Old Testament makes it clear that Israel would forfeit the land if they rebelled against God. Israel's right to the land depended on their living within God's terms.

This same opportunity actually existed for the Canaanite groups already within the land. These groups could *become* Israel. Rahab is a prime example of this. As a prostitute and presumably a worshiper of local deities, she is just the kind of person with whom Israel should have no contact and who should be set aside for destruction (Deuteronomy 7:1-5). Yet, by helping the spies and confessing faith in Yahweh (Joshua 2:8-11), she is saved with her family at Jericho.

The story of Rahab is an extended one in the book of Joshua, showing the importance of her story within the book. A contrasting story within Joshua is the story of Achan. That story is also described at length, highlighting its importance. Although Achan is by birth an Israelite, he forfeits his right to be part of Israel because of his disobedience. Indeed Israel itself later forfeits its right to the land when it becomes disobedient. God then uses the foreign nations of Assyria and Babylon as agents of his judgment on Israel, which has turned its back on him.

What emerges from the broader conquest narrative is thus not at all a tale of ethnic cleansing. Yes, the people of Israel are chosen by God to inherit Canaan. But they will benefit from the land only as long as they remain faithful to God's purposes. The invitation to be part of Israel was open to individuals from those nations who were being dispossessed of the land. Rahab is one example of an individual who took advantage of this opportunity. By the time we reach the land allocation for Israel's twelve tribes, we find that Israel is a far more diverse group then we might have imagined.

It is true that the number of people grafted into Israel is relatively small, as a percentage of the displaced overall population. But it remains true that the opportunity was always there to join with Israel and thereby align with Yahweh's purposes. Further, it was typically the practice of the time that, when invading armies threatened, most of the population would melt away into the hills. In the case of Israel invading Canaan, only those actively opposing God's purposes were killed.

All this does not automatically remove any and all moral difficulties arising from the conquest narrative. But it does set the overall context for this narrative. God wants a people who will be faithful to him. Israel is of course to play this role. But "all Israel" is also described as "foreigners living among them and the native-born" (Joshua 8:33). Israel here is functionally those who have committed themselves to God's purposes.

And what are God's purposes? Recalling our earlier distinction between ultimate goals and intermediate goals, we are asking what God's ultimate purposes are. What are God's ultimate goals in giving the Israelites the land of Canaan? The answer is that God is seeking to reveal himself to the whole world through Israel. They are to be the "light for the Gentiles, that my salvation may reach to the ends of the earth" (Isaiah 49:6). God's full revelation to the world will later come in the person of Jesus Christ. But as part of God's progressive revelation to humankind, God's purpose is to show the world what a relationship with him looks like. God must first teach Israel about the shape of the relationship he wants them to have with him and with one another. As other nations witness this covenantal life with God, they will be drawn into this life as well. From the beginning of Israel's formation, this is God's ultimate goal.

We see the completion of this goal in the book of Revelation, which gives a picture of the great multitude in heaven "from every nation, tribe, people and language, standing before the throne and before the

Lamb" (Revelation 7:9). This ultimate goal is the culmination of the overall biblical narrative. The conquest narrative, as with all subsets of this overall narrative, may describe God's intermediate purposes of giving land to the Israelites, exposing the wickedness of the Canaanites, setting aside Israel to be a light to the nations, and so forth. But all these intermediate purposes serve God's ultimate purpose of drawing people from every tribe and nation into relationship with himself.

Yes, in the conquest narrative there is a clear sense in which the more immediate well-being of the Canaanites is compromised. Perhaps it is right to say that the more immediate well-being of the Israelites is even prioritized over that of the Canaanites. But again, these are not *ultimate* purposes or goals God has. The conquest narrative implies nothing about God's desire or plan for the Canaanites to be among the finally redeemed in heaven.

Elsewhere I have written about the reasons we have for thinking that God will make provisions for every person to receive God's offer of full and final reconciliation—even if explicit knowledge about Christ does not occur until after one's earthly life.[2] The Church has a long history of affirming the possibility of people having, within their earthly lives, "implicit faith" in Christ. This occurs as they respond in various ways to the promptings of the Holy Spirit, even without recognizing that it is the Holy Spirit, or the Spirit of Christ, to whom they are actually responding. They are thereby establishing *some* form of positive relationship with God, given that they are responding positively to God's communication to them. Indeed, we must affirm that Old Testament figures like Noah and Abraham had a kind of implicit faith in Christ. The consensus among the Church Fathers was that these Old Testament saints received the message about Jesus Christ at some point

---

[2]See Kevin Kinghorn, *The Decision of Faith: Can Christian Beliefs Be Freely Chosen?* (London: T & T Clark, 2005), ch. 8; and "The Fate of the 'Good Person'" in *The New Theists*, ed. Josh Rasmussen and Kevin Vallier (London: Routledge, forthcoming).

after their earthly lives and at that time were able to confirm explicitly the moral orientation towards Christ that they developed in their earthly lives as they responded to the light from God available to them. There is no good reason to suppose that what was possible for Noah and Abraham would not be possible for disposed Canaanites.

The conquest narrative thus gives us no reason to suppose that God does not seek the (ultimate) well-being of all people. The main argument of this chapter still stands: God's essential nature as loving implies that he seeks the long-term well-being of every person. The conquest narrative, for all its complexities, can rightly be seen as one of the many subplots within the biblical narrative of God seeking to draw all people to himself, in whom alone we humans find our long-term flourishing. As any parent, teacher, or coach who implements discipline knows, short-term well-being may sometimes need to be compromised in order to best promote long-term flourishing. The conquest narrative is an admittedly complex story involving God's progressive revelation to humankind through the nation of Israel. But for all these complexities, the priority of God's goals remains familiar and simple: intermediate well-being for some people gets compromised for the ultimate goal of bringing deeper, lasting well-being to all of humanity.

I turn now to a second biblical passage commonly used to question God's commitment to the well-being of all people. Romans 9 is often interpreted as a bold statement from Paul on God's choice simply not to favor some people, even his will that they be destroyed. The core of the passage is Romans 9:11-24, and arising from it are a number of interpretive questions—far too many to go through in this book. But I want to focus on a key excerpt, which deals most directly with God's wrath and with the idea that God might have as a goal some people's destruction: Romans 9:22-24.

> What if God, although choosing to show his wrath and make his power known, bore with great patience the objects of his wrath—prepared

for destruction? What if he did this to make the riches of his glory known to the objects of his mercy, whom he prepared in advance for glory—even us, whom he also called, not only from the Jews but also from the Gentiles?

A critical question in interpreting this passage concerns how we should frame the word translated *choosing* at the beginning of the passage. The NIV translators obviously made the decision to begin the passage with "*although* choosing." But there is no word in the original Greek corresponding to *although*. The NIV translators add this as a way of framing the sentence: "*Although* God chooses to show wrath, *yet* he bore with great patience the objects of his wrath." This makes it sound like God's ultimate goal is to demonstrate his wrath, but in the short term he may delay his pursuit of this ultimate goal.

But we could just as easily frame this sentence as follows: "*Because* God chooses to show his wrath, he bore with great patience the objects of his wrath." Framed like this, God's delaying his wrath is *linked with* the demonstration of his wrath. Both the delaying and the demonstrating serve the same ultimate goal. What is that goal?

The entire context of Romans 8–11 is an extended discussion by Paul of the way in which God is grafting the Gentile people into Israel, his chosen people. The Gentiles have witnessed God's blessing on Israel, as well as the folly of those who tried to oppose God. They (or at least some of them) want to embrace the offer of a covenantal relationship, which God has now extended to them, particularly as Israel has failed to be faithful. But of course the original Israel is not discarded forever. Just as the Gentiles were once envious of the special status of Israel, so Israel will now be motivated to turn back to God in part because of what they see God doing though the Gentiles. (Romans 11:11: "Salvation has come to the Gentiles to make Israel envious.")

This has been a complicated history of God revealing, through a particular people, the benefits of a relationship with him, then responding to the unfaithfulness of these people, and then reaching a tipping point in which he must use other people as instruments of further revelation about who he is. Through this process, he has sovereignly chosen Jacob and not Esau (Romans 9:13). He has hardened Pharaoh's heart—or at least brought his hardness of heart more fully to light (Romans 9:17-18). He has designed some people "for special purposes and some for common use" (Romans 9:21). As we saw in looking at the conquest narrative, God also issues judgments on nations, and he at times delays the judgment and destruction that people have brought on themselves by their unrighteousness.

What remains the constant thread is God's ultimate goal of drawing all people to himself, both Israelite and Gentile. (Revelation 7:9: "every nation, tribe, people and language.") Broadly speaking, Romans 9 is best seen as a description of some of the extreme and initially counterintuitive intermediate goals that God pursues—as means toward his ultimate goal of bringing people into the ongoing life of God. More specifically, Romans 9 is part of Paul's larger story of the complementary roles that Israel and the Gentiles are playing in God's grand plan of reconciling the world to himself.

It is crucial in interpreting Romans 9 to remain mindful that this chapter occurs within Paul's larger story of Romans 8–11. The climax of Paul's story occurs at the end of Romans 11. God's final answer is emphatically that *all* are included in God's merciful plans. This conclusion is all the more clear and emphatic precisely because it serves as a contrast to Paul's preceding conditionals and hypotheticals. "What if God has prepared some people for common use or even destruction?" "But didn't God say that he will have mercy on whom he has mercy?" "And didn't God choose Jacob and not Esau?" Paul lists all the arguments which might incline us to think that God does in the end play favorites and have loving plans for some but not others. Yet, the final words of Paul's extended narrative are again as emphatic as they could be: "God has bound *everyone* over to disobedience so that he may have mercy on them *all*" (Romans 11:32). Thus, it turns out that Romans 9 does not offer reasons for thinking that God is selective in extending loving plans to people. Rather, it is part of a larger argument from Paul which makes the very opposite point!

These conclusions from Romans are very much in line with the earlier conclusions about the conquest narrative. At times people's more immediate well-being may be sacrificed as a way of God directing and motivating humanity to turn to himself, in whom alone we humans find our long-term flourishing. Romans 9 need not cause us to revise the main conclusion of this chapter: God's revelation that he loves us as a father must imply that he seeks all people's well-being. It is people's final, eternal well-being that is the nonnegotiable point.

The space constraints of this book again allow me only to explore the conquest narrative and Romans 9. Still, these two narratives seem to me to be the ones most naturally raised against my earlier conclusions in this chapter about God's love. Other narratives might of course be raised, but my responses to them would tend to follow the same broad outline I have already indicated in the discussion of these two examples.

There are of course plenty of other biblical passages that at first reading seem strongly to *support* my conclusions of this chapter: for example, the statement that God is "not wanting anyone to perish, but everyone to come to repentance" (2 Peter 3:9). But my aim in this section was merely to show that the passages that might most naturally be taken to undermine my conclusion do not in the end do so.

Moving Forward

A final reminder of the main takeaway point from this chapter before moving on. Whatever may or may not be included in God's self-disclosure that he loves us as our heavenly Father, one point can be firmly established. God cannot fail to be committed to people's long-term well-being. Benevolence is centrally tied to the concept we have of a loving father. Thus God can rely on this model in communicating the nature of his relationship to us, only if he indeed has a benevolent commitment toward us. These conclusions accord with the overall narrative of Scripture—even with those passages that at first glance may seem most difficult to reconcile with them. So I remain firm in my summary conclusion that God's pattern of actions toward us must be unwaveringly benevolent.

The next question to consider is whether God might have other commitments. Supposing that God is committed to benevolent patterns of action toward all people, might God also have other commitments? Might these other commitments at times clash with his commitment to advance each person's flourishing? What of God's commitment to justice? To holiness? To his own glory? These are the questions to be taken up in the next chapter.

4

LOVE IN RELATION TO JUSTICE, HOLINESS, AND GLORY

T he discussion thus far has led to the conclusion that God is committed to acting in ways consistent with the benevolent goal of furthering people's well-being. I want now to consider whether other divine goals may at times compete with the goal of furthering people's well-being. Specifically, it might be thought that God is committed to outcomes that are just, outcomes that reflect God's holiness, and outcomes that bring God glory.

These three potential commitments are not the only ones a Christian might list as potentially competing commitments to benevolence. But they seem to me the three most commonly cited commitments. I have often heard in sermons: "Yes, God is a God of love—but he is also a God of *justice!*" Or, instead of justice, it is not uncommon to hear, "But he is also a *holy* God." The idea seems to be that love may commend one course of action, but justice or holiness can commend another course of action.

I have found claims about God's glory usually to take the following form: "Demonstrations of God's love are *one* way God is glorified, but they are not the only way." So, for example, it might be thought that God is glorified when perfect justice is realized or when sinful people receive the punishment they deserve. Hence, John Calvin wrote that sinful humans "glorify him by their destruction."[1] And Samuel Hopkins

---

[1] John Calvin, *Institutes of the Christian Religion*, trans. Henry Beveridge (Peabody, MA: Hendrickson, 2008), book III, chap. 23, para. 6.

discussed "whether men ought or can be willing to be damned, if this be necessary for the glory of God and the greatest general good."[2]

In this chapter I want to discuss in turn the relationship divine love has to God's glory, to God's holiness, and to God's justice. Each of these three themes involves particular goals that are thought to have value of some kind. Thus, there is something good, something valuable, about God receiving glory. It would be a worse state of affairs if God did not receive glory. Similarly, it would be a bad thing, perhaps a form of evil, if God were (somehow) not to remain holy. Further, a world with perfect justice would be better, would be more valuable, than a world where injustice is not addressed. Christians will concur that valuable goals are achieved when God executes justice, preserves holiness, and is glorified.

Now, it may turn out that the valued goals associated with justice, holiness, and glory never actually compete with the benevolent goal of humans' well-being. Perhaps these first three valued goals are actually subsumed under, or included within, benevolent love. I am convinced that, on closer analysis, this actually turns out to be the case. But it will take some philosophical argument to show why God's concerns for justice, for his holiness, and for his glory never compete with his benevolent commitment to seek people's well-being at all times. This chapter is devoted to making that argument.

Ultimately my concern in this book is how God's commitment to certain goals might motivate those actions of his we associate with his wrath. The reason I am looking in this chapter so closely at justice, holiness, and glory is that they are sometimes offered as the goals God is seeking to achieve when he acts in wrath. But my aim in this chapter is to show that God's commitments to justice, holiness, and glory are actually included within his benevolent commitment to bring fullness

---

[2]Samuel Hopkins, "Letter to Dr. Ryland," in *The Works of Samuel Hopkins* (Boston: Doctrinal Tract and Book Society, 1852), 2:756.

of life to people. Thus, if we look for the reasons God has for acting in wrath, we must ultimately look at how God's wrath (somehow) plays a role in God seeking to bring fullness of life to people. After all, if the arguments of this chapter are correct, then all of God's actions toward us—including his wrathful ones—will be motivated ultimately by this all-encompassing goal of others' well-being.

Two Ways of Viewing God's Commitments to Us

At this point we must all make a crucial decision. There are two general ways of viewing the relationship God's love has to the three concerns of justice, holiness, and glory. For that matter, there are two general ways of viewing the relationship God's love has to *any* other concerns or commitments God might have. But one of these two ways turns out to be deeply problematic.

On the one hand, we might judge that there exist a number of different, ultimate goals God has when he relates to us—and that the values achieved by these goals are incommensurable. To say that two values are incommensurable is to say that they cannot be compared with one another on some common scale. There is no way to say which value is more valuable.

The problem of incommensurability arises in various contexts in daily life. For instance, people will debate the question: Who is the greatest athlete of the past century? Some may nominate a runner with explosive speed, such as Jesse Owens (four gold medals at the 1936 Olympics) or Usain Bolt (current record holder at 100 and 200 meters). But how does explosive speed compare with the stamina of a long-distance runner such as Haile Gebrselassie (two Olympic golds at 10,000 meters and former marathon record holder)? What about a versatile athlete who combined speed, stamina, and power, such as Jim Thorpe (Olympic gold medalist and professional baseball, basketball, and American football player)? Of course, a ballerina such as

Natalia Osipova (YouTube her!) also exhibits these qualities, while also retaining elegant body control. In short, the obvious answer to the question of the greatest athlete is that there simply is no single answer. A variety of athletic traits exist, and there is no way to say which trait is more athletic than another.

Similarly, the Christian might conclude that benevolent goals are neither more nor less valuable than the goals of justice, holiness, and divine glory. They are all worthy pursuits, and it is simply impossible to compare on some common scale the values associated with them.

The second way of viewing them is to conclude that they *can* be compared in some manner, with perhaps some valued goals being subsumed under other valued goals. My larger argument in this chapter is to show why this second option makes sense—and why the goals of justice, holiness, and divine glory could never actually compete with God's benevolent commitments. But first, let me say why it is so problematic to view the goals we have been considering as incommensurable in value.

The easiest way of putting the problem may sound a bit frivolous at first hearing. But the problem really is quite a serious one. The simplest way of putting it is as follows. Suppose that God is committed to pursuing the benevolent end of our well-being. Suppose that God is also committed to pursuing the end of justice (or holiness or divine glory). Suppose that the values within these goals are incommensurable. Well, the pursuit of benevolence may require one action, with the pursuit of justice requiring a different action. When we pray to God about a situation in our lives, which ultimate goal—our well-being or justice—will God be committed to pursuing? The only answer could be: it depends on what day you catch him.

This again may seem a frivolous way of putting the point. But the point is quite a significant one. The steadfastness of God's love for us is at stake, as well as the stability of God's essential character. Surely it is preposterous to suggest that God would be more concerned with justice than with our well-being one day, but more concerned with our well-being than with justice the next day. Such priority of commitment must surely be settled as part of God having a constant, single moral character.

Presumably there are some matters, not related to one's essential moral character, that are subject to change and to personal preference at a given time. For instance, we humans have an aesthetic appreciation for the beauty of oceans and mountains. Some days we may prefer to look at a picture of an ocean, and other days we may prefer a mountain scene. Supposing that the human capacity to appreciate beauty reflects certain attributes of God, we can imagine that God could enjoy contemplating the beauty of oceans and mountains he has created. Perhaps on some occasions God prefers to contemplate the beauty of oceans and on other occasions prefers to contemplate the beauty of mountains. I say "perhaps" to indicate that there seems no theological reason, linked to God's essential character, that would preclude God having different preferences at different times on such matters as aesthetic taste.

Still, the point remains that commitments to goals such as justice or human well-being reflect one's core, moral commitments. If, as I have already argued, God's benevolent commitment to our well-being is steadfast, then how are we to view God's commitments to justice, to holiness, and to his own glory? Can these further commitments be reconciled to God's commitment of love, perhaps coming under the umbrella of God's essential commitment of love? I think they indeed can be. I want to outline a way of viewing these three further commitments *in terms of* God's love. Let me begin with the matter of God's glory.

LOVE AND GOD'S GLORY

There are interesting questions one might explore about God's glory, such as whether we can contribute to God's glory (for instance, as the psalmist blesses or praises the Lord, as in Psalm 103:1) or whether God's glory is simply something that is uncovered (as when God's glory passes by Moses in Exodus 33:22). Perhaps the term *glory* has various facets as it is used throughout the Bible. But as a general point, God's glory seems to involve some aspect of God being made clear: his character, his power, his beauty, and so forth. If this is so, then God's glory will be linked heavily with God's love. After all, as discussed in chapter two, the Christian doctrine of God centers on the manner in which God is love: three persons in eternal, interdependent relationships of self-giving. If God is glorified as some aspect of his character is made clear, and if God's eternal and essential trinitarian character is love, then wouldn't revealing God's glory inevitably involve revealing something of God's love? It seems difficult to imagine that God's glory might shine through in some context without God's love also shining through. At the very least, it is impossible that any demonstration of God's glory could come in contrast to God's love, which once again is an essential attribute at the very heart of who God is.

This link between divine glory and divine love accords well with Jesus' extended prayer in the Gospel of John, which seems clearly to link glory and love. Jesus prays to the Father, "Glorify your Son, that your Son may glorify you" (John 17:1). He extends his prayer for glory to those people in the world who belong to him, "that all of them may be one, Father, just as you are in me and I am in you. . . . I have given them the glory that you gave me, that they may be one as we are one" (John 17:21-22). There thus seems to be a clear connection between participating in God's glory and participating in the *life* of God, in which unity is achieved through the loving, interdependent relationships that, once again, are at the core of the Christian doctrine of the Trinity. In short, God's glory is demonstrated as persons participate in God-centered relationships of self-giving love, which for us humans is to arrive at fullness of life.

What of the idea that God might be glorified when people are eternally separated from him, receiving the inevitable consequences they deserve through their rejection of God? Well, there perhaps is a sense in which God's glory is revealed through this event—although it only reaffirms the links among glory, love, and fullness of life. The plight of those separated from God highlights that God is indeed the sole source of joy, peace, freedom, and so forth. This role of God as the source of life itself becomes all the more abundantly clear. Further, God's sorrow at the self-destructive choices of those he loves—which surely is the only appropriate emotion for a God of love—highlights his deep desire that people choose to embrace his offer of fullness of life with him for eternity.

This sense of how God can receive glory is a far cry from the idea that God is glorified when his perfect will that some persons suffer eternal separation from him is achieved. God's willing that some people suffer eternal separation is clearly not consistent with benevolent love, for reasons I outlined in chapter three. If the claim were made that God receives glory when his will for a person's eternal separation is achieved, it would clearly have to be something *other* than, and *contrary to*, God's benevolent love that would have been revealed. But of course all this is impossible, given the premise that God is essentially love (chapter two) and the premise that God's revealed love to us is necessarily tied to a commitment to all people's well-being (chapter three).

I have been highlighting a quite different sense in which God can be said to receive glory when people are eternally separated from him. It is not that he is glorified as he wills for people to be separated. Rather, he is glorified as his benevolent desires for all people's well-being are revealed. This revealed desire, of course, is so often expressed through Scripture in terms of God's lament and sorrow when the people he loves turn from him and head toward the path of self-destruction.

In short, there is no reason to think that considerations of God's glory might compete with the benevolent goal God has that we come to share in his abundant life. God is glorified when the people he loves receive fullness of life by participating in perfected relationships with God and with others in whom God's Spirit dwells. God could never be glorified at the expense of his essential attribute of benevolent love. Rather, God is glorified precisely as his essential character of love is revealed in his benevolent pursuit of others' well-being.

LOVE AND GOD'S HOLINESS

Let me move now to considerations of God's holiness. As discussed in chapter two, within the Bible holiness is a way of describing the uniqueness or otherness of God. Whatever attributes God has, his holiness is a reminder that these attributes will, in some ways, remain different from anything else in the created order. In terms of moral attributes, to say that God is holy is not yet to say what his moral attributes *are*. It is just to say that these attributes will in some ways be different from ours.

If we look at God's essential attribute of benevolent love, to say that God has holy love is to say that God's love is in a class by itself. That is, no human can remotely match the extent of God's benevolent commitment to us. Christ in humility took on human form, led a perfect life through temptation and suffering, and died for the sake of the very ones who nailed him to a cross. This humble initiative to woo lesser people who have their backs to him is unmatched by any human. So is the willingness, without exception, to absorb the costs of others' follies. So is the patient and long-suffering commitment to love stubborn people and to keep loving them until they're lovable. Yes, following the arguments of chapter three, God's love must bear *some* important similarities to the best human examples by which we learn the concept of love. (Otherwise, we would be at a loss to understand

God's revelation to us that he loves us.) Nevertheless, God's love remains unique, unmatched, other than any example of human love.

This discussion of God's holy love obviously does nothing to suggest that God's holiness, his otherness, might compete with his commitment to benevolent love. Nevertheless, we noted in chapter two that a particular attribute of God often associated with God's holiness, or otherness, is God's purity. God is in every way separate from sin. He can in no way approve of sin or turn a blind eye to it.

When God's holiness is thought of in terms of God's purity, it perhaps makes sense to wonder if God's holiness is potentially at odds with God's love. I again have heard in plenty of sermons: "Yes, God is a God of love, *but* he is also a holy God." Why would one juxtapose love and holiness in this manner? I suspect the idea is that love inevitably lapses into *permissiveness* unless it is "balanced" by holiness. In other words, God's purity demands that he take an uncompromising stance on sin, that he refuse to sugarcoat people's predicaments, that he pronounce the truth to people of their immorality. If we affirm God's love without also affirming God's holiness (i.e., God's uncompromising posture against sin), then God's love can quickly degenerate into permissiveness and indulgence.

But why characterize love, by itself, in terms of permissiveness? If I (over)indulge a person, believing that the person as a result will not be better off in the long term, I have not acted out of benevolent love. Ironically, permissiveness usually reveals a clear preference for self over concern for the other person. After all, why would a parent forgo disciplining a child? Why would someone not want to confront a friend with tough love, even while recognizing that the friend needs to be confronted?

Perhaps in some cases it is simply that we are very unwise. Or perhaps it is better to say that we are very imprudent. We are focused merely on the other person's immediate or short-term happiness. We are giving no real thought to the person's long-term need to develop the kind of character that would eventually lead him or her to a much deeper life of joy and peace. But I suspect in most cases we actually recognize that we're not doing the other person any long-term favors. If so, then why would we refrain in some instance from disciplining a child or confronting a friend? Because it's uncomfortable.

It's an effort at times not to simply give in to a child's demands. When we say no, we know the child is going to be upset. There might even be a public scene. Also, if we discipline our child then we're going to have to have the long talk with the child about "how this is really for your own long-term good," about "how this hurts me more than it hurts you," and so on. There's a lot of time and emotional energy expended in disciplining a child. It's much easier just to give in to the child and forgo the discipline. But is that ever the loving thing to do, when we believe our child really does need disciplining? Obviously not. Our failure to do so is because we don't want to take the time and effort. It's an inconvenience, a bother to us. We prefer our own well-being to the well-being of our child. An overly permissive parent doesn't demonstrate the pitfalls of loving too much and without restraint. Rather, such a parent demonstrates the failure of loving too little.

A similar thing could be said of the failure to confront a friend with a difficult truth. Now, perhaps sometimes we may refrain from confronting a friend because we know the friend at present is emotionally fragile. The friend may genuinely not be in a position to hear and receive the truth without being permanently crushed. In such cases, we might refrain from confronting the friend out of genuine, loving concern.

But often times we may know that a friend really does need to be challenged about some behavior of theirs. We know it is in the friend's long-term, best interest to be confronted. In these cases, why would we fail to do so? Our permissiveness is again easy to understand. It's uncomfortable to confront other people! There's a huge amount of emotional energy expended. And what if the other person doesn't receive it well? What if the other person turns on me and I end up losing this friendship? It can be downright scary to confront a friend with a really difficult truth. But if we genuinely believe that a friend needs to be confronted, for his or her own long-term good, could a failure to confront the friend ever be described as a benevolent response? If we genuinely believe that, by not confronting a friend, the friend will be comparatively worse off in the long run, could permissiveness be a form of love for the friend? Obviously not. Permissiveness in such situations reveals a *self-interested* desire to avoid uncomfortable and risky confrontation—not a benevolent desire for the friend's well-being.

Love, properly understood, does not lead to us to ignore others' sins and moral shortcomings. It does not lead to undue permissiveness. Quite the opposite. Undue permissiveness typically reveals a self-interested preference to be comfortable at the expense of what we know to be someone else's long-term flourishing. Such permissiveness is thus in direct contrast to a commitment of benevolent love. So we need not claim that "God is a God of love, *but also* a holy God who cannot countenance sin." An affirmation of God's purity is already subsumed within the idea that God acts at all times out of the motivation of benevolent love. Are there other reasons for thinking that benevolent love could not motivate all of God's actions toward us? Let me turn to the claim that God's actions must be just in addition to being loving.

LOVE AND GOD'S JUSTICE

There are some thoughtful arguments for the idea that God must be motivated not only by love but also by concerns for justice. My conclusion will be that these arguments don't ultimately work. But I want to consider them closely in this section.

Must love be tempered by, or balanced with, justice? This has certainly been the claim of various Christian ethicists and theologians. Swiss theologian Emil Brunner warned that love, if unchecked by justice, soon drifts into sentimentality. Why should this be so? Here is Brunner's answer: "Love which is not just in the world of institutions is sentimentality. And sentimentality, feeling for feeling's sake, is the poison, the solvent that destroys all just institutions."[3]

Brunner is making the point that, as a practical matter in our world, we will need institutions that enforce rules of law so that each person gets his or her due. Loving others involves having affectionate feelings toward them. But there must be something to *guide* these feelings of affection if we want truly good outcomes. Yes, we may love every competitor in a race, but we cannot award a gold medal to every competitor. Yes, we may want every child in elementary school to thrive, but not every child's transcript can reflect grades that are "well above the class average." If we are to have any way of giving people what they truly deserve, then we will need guidelines or rules or laws in place. And Brunner emphasizes that we humans will need institutions that establish and enforce these rules and laws. Just outcomes are important, and they will not be reached if we are merely guided by love.

I want to make two responses to Brunner. First, it is worth considering the general question of what ultimately justifies our laws and institutions. Why do we think we need a court system to enforce rules of law? For that matter, why do we think rules of law are needed in the first place? The obvious answer is that we believe that these things ensure opportunities for people to flourish. Our concern for people within a society leads us to write laws and erect institutions that administer these laws justly. Is there any reason to think that God's

---

[3]Emil Brunner, *Justice and the Social Order* (Cambridge, UK: Lutterworth, 1945), 117.

administration of justice would ultimately be for reasons other than this same benevolent goal that people flourish?

Second, I would argue that love, if properly understood and applied, actually *does* preserve the just outcomes of our valued institutions. This point seems obvious in cases of schools and athletic competitions. After all, to award high grades to students who didn't earn them would be to perpetuate widespread lies: to the students, parents, and school administrators who might look at these student transcripts in the future. Love for others is clearly not consistent with this kind of blatant bad faith toward them. Plus, there is the point that we would very quickly dissolve academic institutions in general, thereby preventing future students from benefitting from the current opportunities they provide. Similar points could be made about athletic competitions.

But I do not want to be too quick in dismissing the claim that there are some cases where love simply does not allow us to find the best outcome, and we must therefore appeal to justice. Christian ethicist Dennis Hollinger discusses an interesting example involving Mickey Mantle, who apparently was given a liver transplant late in his life, even though questions can be raised about whether there were more deserving patients on the transplant list at the time. Hollinger concludes from this example that "love will not solve the moral quandary surrounding organ transplants";[4] instead, we must consider what justice demands.

But do we really have no way of adjudicating the matter of organ transplants if we appeal merely to love? Let us suppose for the sake of argument that, when Mickey Mantle was given a liver transplant, there were more deserving patients needing transplants. In this case, would not the failure to give these patients transplants reveal a lack of

---

[4]Dennis Hollinger, *Choosing the Good: Christian Ethics in a Complex World* (Grand Rapids: Baker Academic, 2002), 221.

love for all people? Would it not reveal a prejudice against those who are not rich or not famous? Could a doctor be said to value the lives of all his patients if he allocated limited resources on a basis other than the medical considerations of patients' age, level of health crisis, and so forth? Could we as citizens be said to care about all our fellow citizens if we did not honor our agreements to one another, which we make explicit in laws about how liver transplant lists are to be ordered? In short, an appeal to love *does* allow us to say why a person who is most deserving of some treatment should receive that treatment. If Mickey Mantle was given undue preferential treatment, we might describe this event in various ways (including failed justice). But ultimately it was a failure to love perfectly.

Admittedly, we are sometimes given by God particular people to prioritize. For instance, it is good that a married couple prioritize each other and any children they have—by spending more time with them, spending more resources on them, championing their causes, and so on. The couple may try to follow Jesus in loving all people throughout the world. But there are certain roles as spouse and parent that they are uniquely able to play. They should perform these roles, which require them to prioritize family members. Yet, this is decidedly not the situation of doctors who decide transplant cases. Perfect love in this case surely means that a doctor will view all his or her patients as bearers of God's image who have families who love them, spiritual gifts that can be put to use for God's kingdom, and so on. Prioritizing a celebrity on a transplant list would again be a failure to love perfectly. That is, it would be a failure to commit to the well-being of all those God has put in our path to love.

A similar point can be made in response to a concern of Christian ethicist Arthur Holmes. Holmes sees problems with an ethic rooted entirely in the pursuit of good consequences, including the consequence of other people's flourishing.

If love is regarded as a consequentialist principle, then it needs to ground the principle of distributive justice on more than simple utility. Indeed, "do unto others as you would have them do to you" sounds equitable and just as well as loving. God is not only loving; he is also just. These two attributes stand out through the entire biblical record, and neither is reducible to the other. I therefore find attempts at a Christian utilitarianism ill begotten; we need an independent principle of justice to ensure an equitable distribution of good, in addition to the principle of love or benevolence that maximizes good consequences.[5]

Holmes makes some thoughtful points here. But should we follow him in concluding that justice is not reducible to love? That is, should we conclude that a concern about what is just cannot be fully explained in terms of a loving concern for others' well-being? This seems the wrong conclusion.

As a starting point in response to Holmes, I would point again to the Mickey Mantle example. If we fail to seek the well-being of all those God has put in our paths to care for, then this is a failure to love perfectly. The instruction to "do to others what you would have them do to you" (Matthew 7:12) is an instruction not to prioritize oneself over others. The same principle of not prioritizing self-interest over benevolence undergirds Jesus's instruction to "love your neighbor as yourself" (Mark 12:31). If we base our treatment of others on the level of personal regard for their celebrity, this is not loving people as shared bearers of God's image.

So, if we give a liver transplant to a celebrity instead of another person who was more deserving by objective, medical criteria, is this is failure to be just? Well, yes. But it can also be described as a failure to love perfectly. There is no need to *balance* perfect love here with justice. In fully loving others we end up doing those very actions that can also be described as just. Holmes notes at one point that "love is

---

[5] Arthur Holmes, *Ethics*, 2nd ed. (Downers Grove, IL: IVP Academic, 2007), 52.

obligated in justice to distribute its benefits equitably, rather than playing favorites or practicing discrimination and unfairness."[6] But love that is truly and fully benevolent will already manifest itself in ways that are equitable.

Continuing Holmes's line of argument, he concludes in the passage above that "we need an independent principle of justice to ensure an equitable distribution of good." My response has again been that loving others fully will manifest itself in concern for the well-being of all people God puts in our paths. But perhaps Holmes will point out that, even if we do have a concern for all people, we still will often not know how to distribute resources. He remarks, "Justice stresses the right outward ordering of life, while love is more an inner, personalized concern. Love without justice would be amorphous and lack direction."[7] Yes, in the Mickie Mantle case we know that a concern for all people will lead us to place the most deserving patient at the top of the liver transplant list. But not every case is this straightforward in terms of what the right thing to do is, as we try to love all people.

Everyone has had that warm feeling of wanting somehow to help others but not knowing exactly how to do it. It's interesting to watch people's acceptance speeches at award ceremonies. The winner often blurts out things like, "I'm just so thankful for everyone in my life," or, "I just love you all so much." It has also been common, to the point of cliché, to express the desire for "world peace." We've all experienced those feelings of love for others, perhaps for the whole world—but we're unsure how to direct our affections of love. Is something else needed to direct our impulses to love others? Justice, perhaps?

The right answer seems to be that something else is indeed needed. But it's not ultimately justice. What's needed are actually two

---

[6]Holmes, *Ethics*, 54.
[7]Holmes, *Ethics*, 54-55.

complementary pieces. First, one needs God's direction. There exists within Christianity a long history of emphasizing one's calling, or vocation. God alone can coordinate all people's well-being so that our commitment to one person's well-being does not come at the expense of another person's ultimate well-being. Every person can fulfill certain divinely appointed tasks in this life and can experience a relationship with God that leads to his or her ultimate and eternal flourishing in heaven. Again, God alone is capable of coordinating all people's well-being in this way. So, if we want our loving impulses to translate to genuine beneficence, where all people are helped and no one is left out, our first need is information about our calling before the Lord. Given our own limited time and resources, we cannot help everyone—at least, not in the same way. But we can work toward the well-being of particular people, which God calls us to do as part of his broader coordinating effort to bring life to all people.

A second need we may have, in order to give direction to affective impulses of love for others, is simply the ability to engage in practical reasoning. This is the kind of reasoning we have to do when we implement plans and seek to achieve goals. We may be in a situation in which we believe God has called us to focus on the well-being of a particular person, for example a work colleague. But how can we best help this person? If God's call to help this person hasn't included all the specific instructions we need, then we must resort to our own practical reasoning. That is, it is partly up to us to think through how we can creatively help meet the needs the other person has.

Both these needed elements—practical reasoning and insight into God's calling—are kinds of knowledge we need. What must direct our loving impulses toward others is not some demand of justice. For one thing, as we saw in chapter two, there are a variety of different ideals that can go by the name "justice": distributive justice, restorative justice, and so forth. If God calls us to prioritize in unique ways the well-being of one of our children, is this justice giving direction to our inward affections? Well, perhaps this depends on what one means by justice. But no appeal to justice (of whatever kind) is actually needed in order for our love for others to translate into acts of beneficence that are equitable for all people. What is fundamentally needed is knowledge about what God has called us to do, as part of his coordinating efforts to bring fullness of life to all people. And we need practical knowledge at times about how best to fulfill our calling before the Lord.

Turning to the question of what guides God's actions, does God ever need to be guided by justice? Well, he already possesses the two kinds of knowledge just discussed. He obviously knows what his own coordinating plans are. As for practical knowledge—about the actions that can best promote people's true well-being—God obviously has that knowledge in spades. So I find no reason for thinking that justice must be added to, or balanced with, God's love in order to give God's actions direction. God will never be at a loss about what to do in furthering people's well-being. God will work toward the goal of furthering all people's well-being, with every person receiving the opportunity to attain fullness of life eternally.

In short, I am not arguing against the idea that God's actions are just. Rather, I am pointing out that God's actions are not ultimately explained by some principle of justice. They are ultimately explained by the benevolent commitment God has toward the people he created. Yes, God's commitments will further the cause of justice. But just actions and outcomes are simply expressions of God's perfect love. Justice need not be seen as an important aspect of God's character *in addition to* God's love. Rather, justice is subsumed under the broader commitment of God's benevolent love toward people.

Situations exist in our world in which one person oppresses another, or cheats another, or falsely accuses another. In these contexts, the most loving act God could perform—both for the victim and for the aggressor—may well be to dispense justice. God may help establish human institutions that administer this justice. For victims, relief is needed from shackles of some kind that are preventing fullness of life for them. For oppressors, their most pressing need is to be stopped in their tracks, as this is the needed first step for them to come eventually to participate in the life of God. Still, God's commitment to justice stems from his loving concern that individuals and communities flourish. Justice is thus one expression of God's love.

I say that justice is *one* expression of God's love. In other contexts, God's mercy will be the appropriate expression of God's love. The same goes for God's leniency, patience, correction, discipline, and so forth. All these ways of relating to people can be seen as appropriate means, depending on the context, of achieving God's ultimate, benevolent goal of drawing people into right relationship with himself, which alone provides them with fullness of life. (Any parent will recognize that sometimes our children need the motivation of a carrot and sometimes the motivation of a stick, so to speak.) To repeat, God relates to us with the constant motivation of benevolent love: seeking our final, eternal well-being at all times. God sometimes acts with mercy, leniency, and patience; he sometimes acts with correction, discipline, and justice. But all these acts are expressions of this same, constant, divine motivation of love—a love that gets expressed in different contexts but remains steadfast in the purpose of drawing people to himself.

Moving Forward

In this current chapter I have considered the question of whether God might also have, in addition to the pursuit of people's well-being, other pursuits which may at times compete with that benevolent goal. I have argued that the answer must be no. Pursuits of justice, mercy, and so forth end up being subsumed under the broader and more fundamental benevolent goal of bringing life to all people. Happily, with this conclusion we avoid the problem of incommensurability: God sometimes acting benevolently toward us but at other times perhaps prioritizing other ways of relating to us that run contrary to love. God may well have concerns of justice, holiness, and divine glory. But these concerns never compete with his benevolent motivation that people flourish in the long term. God's essential character is a stable one, and it is a character of love.

But now I face some challenging questions having to do with God's wrath. Consistent with the conclusions of this chapter, expressions of divine wrath must likewise be for the ultimate, benevolent purpose God has of drawing people into relationship with himself, thereby bringing fullness of life to them. But how exactly are expressions of wrath supposed to accomplish this goal of prompting people to turn to God? Can the stark biblical imagery surrounding divine wrath really be reconciled with the idea that wrath is an expression of benevolent love in a particular context? These are the questions I will pursue in the remaining chapters.

5

WRATH AS GOD PRESSING
THE TRUTH ON US

I concluded the last chapter by saying that God's displays of justice, mercy, patience, discipline, and so forth are demonstrations of love, in differing contexts. At certain times for certain people, God's patience may be the best means of encouraging them to turn to him. In other situations, God's discipline may be the best means. Can God's wrath sometimes be the best means? My conclusion is that the answer is yes. But in showing why this is the case, we first need a clearer understanding of what exactly it means for God to act in wrath.

I noted in chapter one that God's wrath involves a pattern of action designed at some purposeful goal. We have since seen that this goal must (somehow) be a benevolent one, aimed at people's long-term well-being. But this pattern of action—like all patterns of action—will have a certain shape to it. That is, there will be certain features of this pattern that can help us better to understand it. When God acts in wrath, there will be a certain experience humans have as they encounter it. I want to explore these points in this chapter, concluding with a final description of what it means for God to act in wrath.

The Provisional Shape of Divine Wrath

Within the biblical references to divine wrath, we find recurring themes that help us see the shape, or features, of this wrath. In short, we find that God's wrath is intended to be provisional. I briefly made the point in chapter two that the Bible describes limits to God's wrath, in contrast to the constancy of God's love. But I want to say more here about this limited, provisional aspect of divine wrath, which comes through in the biblical narrative in at least three ways. First, we find that God's wrath is always a last resort. Second, we find that God's intent is not that his wrath be the final word. Third, we find that God indeed abandons his wrathful pursuits when repentance occurs.

When God proclaims his name to Moses, he declares himself as being "slow to anger," even while "abounding in love and faithfulness" (Exodus 34:6). This description of God as slow to anger recurs throughout the Old Testament period and in different kinds of books: histories (Numbers 14:18; Nehemiah 9:17), poetry (Psalms 86:15; 103:8; 145:8), prophets (Joel 2:13; Jonah 4:2; Nahum 1:3). This theme of covenantal love and slowness to anger is constantly the basis of God's action in the story of Israel.

The psalmist recounts how God delivered the Israelites from Egypt, only to have the people grumble and rebel against him. Yet, despite the way in which "they were not faithful to his covenant" (Psalm 78:37), the psalmist tells that "time after time he restrained his anger and did not stir up his full wrath" (Psalm 78:38). Similarly, the prophet Ezekiel runs through Israel's history from their time in Egypt onwards, showing how they continually were unfaithful to God, even while God repeatedly withheld his wrath (Ezekiel 20:8-9, 13-14, 21-22). The whole sequence of Israel's failures in Ezekiel 20 reveals them to be a nation virtually incapable of repentance. They are locked into a pattern of sin that persists through the generations. Only through the chastening experience of exile, with other nations carrying out God's wrath against his people, will this pattern be broken. God's wrath is eventually expressed, but it was the very last resort.

We sometimes find God looking for a reason, any reason, to withhold his wrath. Jeremiah records God's instruction to

Go up and down the streets of Jerusalem,
 look around and consider,
 search through her squares.
If you can find but one person
 who deals honestly and seeks the truth,
 I will forgive this city. (Jeremiah 5:1)

God similarly invites Abraham to intercede on behalf of Sodom, eventually declaring that "For the sake of ten, I will not destroy it" (Genesis 18:32). Again, wrath is God's last resort to people's sin and unfaithfulness, his final plan when all other strategies are exhausted. As a good summation of this general point, 2 Chronicles 36:16 records how "the wrath of the LORD was aroused against his people"—but only after his people had "mocked God's messengers, despised his words and scoffed at his prophets" until "there was no remedy."

When God does finally act in wrath, we find throughout Scripture that it is not intended to be his final word. For example, in Jeremiah 5, after an extended description of the destruction God will bring about in response to his people's continued wickedness, God declares, "Yet even in those days . . . I will not destroy you completely" (Jeremiah 5:18). This language—of God acting in wrath, *and yet* in the end showing compassion—recurs throughout the Old Testament in God's dealings with his people. The Lord warns through Ezekiel: "I will deal with you as you deserve, because you have despised my oath by breaking the covenant. *Yet* I will remember the covenant I made with you in the days of your youth, and I will establish an everlasting covenant with you" (Ezekiel 16:59-60). Through the sadness of Lamentations, we hear the reminder that "*Though* he brings grief, he will show compassion, so great is his unfailing love. For he does not willingly bring affliction or grief to anyone" (Lamentations 3:32-33).

Even at the most hopeless point of exile, the seemingly final act of God's judgment on his people, God shares the promise of some future time. We read in Hosea how Ephraim has "aroused his bitter anger" (Hosea 12:14), which is the reason the Lord "will pour out my wrath on them like a flood of water" (Hosea 5:10). The situation looks hopeless, just as the state of Hosea's marriage looks hopeless. Disaster will come on the present generation in the form of an Assyrian invasion. But that is not God's last word. Just as the marriage of Hosea and Gomer will make a fresh start (Hosea 3:1-3), so Israel will make a fresh start with God (Hosea 3:4-5). The God who says, "I will no longer love them" (Hosea 9:15) also says, "I will heal their waywardness and love them freely, for my anger has turned away from them" (Hosea 14:4).

When even Jerusalem rebels against God to the point that there is "no remedy" (2 Chronicles 36:16), God brings "against them the king of the Babylonians" and gives them "all into the hands of Nebuchadnezzar" (2 Chronicles 36:17). Yet, God does not give up on his people. A remnant is preserved in Babylon until the time when "the LORD moved the heart of Cyrus king of Persia" (2 Chronicles 36:22), and Cyrus permits Jewish people to return to Judah. In issuing this decree, Cyrus is also moved to proclaim the blessing: "and may the LORD their God be with them" (2 Chronicles 36:23).

This restoration of God's people is of course only part of a larger restoration, a day of the Lord, in which God will establish an "everlasting covenant" (Ezekiel 16:60) with his people. How will this final restoration come about? Ezekiel explains that it will not come through Judah's national leaders, the "shepherds of Israel" (Ezekiel 34:2), for they have failed so completely to lead the people—the flock—in God's ways. Indeed, the shepherds have "cared for themselves rather than for my flock" (Ezekiel 34:8) and have even fed themselves (Ezekiel 34:10) on the flock. God himself must rescue and protect them: "I myself will search for my sheep and look after them" (Ezekiel 34:11). God also points to the time in which "I will place over them one shepherd, my servant David, and he will tend them; he will tend them and be their shepherd" (Ezekiel 34:23). This reference to "one shepherd, my servant David," presiding over the flock suggests a future, ideal king, descended from David and presiding over reunited Israel and Judah. We know from Isaiah that "He will reign on David's throne and over his kingdom, establishing and upholding it with justice and righteousness from that time on and forever" (Isaiah 9:7).

In the light of the New Testament we recognize this person as Jesus Christ, who provides the way for full and final reconciliation with God and for restoration for his people. Yes, "we were by nature deserving of wrath" (Ephesians 2:3). This is our situation apart from Christ. But now God has "made us alive with Christ" (Ephesians 2:5) as we turn to Christ in faith, making him lord of our lives.

In the structure of Romans, the warning of God's wrath (Romans 1:18) follows immediately and is juxtaposed with the announcement of the gospel of justification through faith (Romans 1:16-17). God's opposition to people's sin exposes them to his wrath, but he offers in Christ the way of deliverance from wrath. In Christ, God himself absorbs the destructive consequences of sin. And of course the restoration Christ offers to those who follow him is an everlasting one.

This theme of people being no longer subject to God's wrath, if they only repent and turn to him, is a continuation of the Old Testament narrative of God abandoning wrath when repentance occurs. When the Israelites stand on the verge of entering the Promised Land, Moses looks ahead to the time when the people will provoke God to the point that "his wrath and zeal will burn against them" (Deuteronomy 29:20). "In furious anger and in great wrath" God will uproot them from their land and "thrust them into another land" (Deuteronomy 29:28). Even so, Moses confirms that "when you and your children return to the LORD your God and obey him with all your heart," God will "restore your fortunes and have compassion on you and gather you again from all the nations where he scattered you" (Deuteronomy 30:2-3). Moses here is really just reiterating the familiar theme of God setting before people "life and death, blessings and curses," and he is exhorting the people to choose life (Deuteronomy 30:19).

God's word through Jeremiah offers the broadest summary of this theme: "If at any time I announce that a nation or kingdom is to be uprooted, torn down and destroyed, and if that nation I warned repents of its evil, then I will relent and not inflict on it the disaster I had planned" (Jeremiah 18:7-8). Further, God explicitly tells Jeremiah why he is to write down all his prophecies: "Perhaps when the people of Judah hear about every disaster I plan to inflict on them, they will each turn from their wicked ways; then I will forgive their wickedness and their sin" (Jeremiah 36:3).

It is impossible to read God's interactions with his people *without* assuming the implicit promise to abandon his wrath, if and when his people turn to him. The psalmist urges those around him to listen to God's voice, which calls out, "Do not harden your hearts as you did at Meribah, as you did that day at Massah in the wilderness, where your ancestors tested me" (Psalm 95:8-9). This warning of course implies a promise. God's wrath is not inevitable or permanent. The people are not locked into a cycle of decline or subjection to other nations. They are free to choose another destiny. God can be counted on to meet them faithfully when they turn to him.

To sum up this section, three features of divine wrath come through consistently within the biblical narrative: (1) God's wrath occurs as a final response to people's offenses, a response of last resort; (2) God's intent is that his wrath not be the final word; and (3) God stands ready to abandon his wrathful actions whenever this further goal—linked to human repentance—comes to fruition. In short, the biblical narrative indicates that God's wrath has a *provisional* shape to it, something that ideally is not meant to last.

God's Wrath as a Kind of Action

I want to move now to the specific kind of action God is performing when he acts in wrath. We have seen from Scripture that God's acts of wrath are intended to be provisional. But what exactly is God doing when he acts in wrath? What is the best description of the kind of action God is performing when he acts in wrath?

By asking about the kind of action God is performing, I am asking about the most basic description of those actions we characterize as wrathful ones. To illustrate, a military general may issue a command to a platoon of soldiers. Now, the general may issue this command in order to position troops strategically. The new positions of the troops may be needed in order to win a battle, and the battle may serve the larger purpose of winning the war, and the war may be fought in order to achieve the final, ultimate goal of preserving the safety of the country's citizens. The general may have all these goals in mind when issuing a command. His action before his troops might be described in terms of positioning troops strategically, or plotting a victory in battle, or acting to protect a country's citizens. But again the initial action itself is the action of issuing a command. That's the barest, most basic description of the general's action in this instance.

Other kinds of action include asking a question, giving an answer, reminding someone of a promise, declaring something a forgery, accusing someone of a lie, lifting a chair, squeezing someone's wrist, and so on. These are kinds of actions people can perform. Of course, there are inevitably further, longer-term goals we have when we perform intentional actions such as these. From our previous look at the provisional shape of divine wrath throughout Scripture, God will seemingly have further, longer-term goals when he acts in wrath. But I am now asking the question of what the barest, most basic description is of those actions associated with God's wrath. What kind of action is an act of wrath?

In answering this question perhaps the best place to begin is with our experiences of being on the receiving end of divine wrath. Our experiences of others' actions often give us huge insight into the kinds of actions they are in fact performing. For instance, it feels very different to be given an answer than to be asked a question. These are two different types of actions other people can perform; and we know the difference between the two partly because of the different experiences we have as the target of these actions. When we are given an answer to some question, we can relax and just absorb the information. But when we are asked a question, we immediately feel we have to do something. The onus is on us to respond in some way.

There are any number of similar examples in which we gain insight into the kind of action someone is performing by reflecting on our experience of being on the receiving end of that action. Declarations and accusations are different kinds of actions. We know their difference largely by reflecting on the very different ways those actions feel to us. If someone declares that we have a nice car, they may be making polite conversation or even admiring our choices. But if someone accuses us of having a nice car, then suddenly we find ourselves facing up to the question of whether we have done something wrong—perhaps used our money irresponsibly or failed to give to others in need. Again, the experience of being on the receiving end of someone's action is heavily tied to the *kind* of action that person has in fact performed. What is the experience like of being on the receiving end of God's wrath?

Obviously, the imagery in Scripture is that it is an unpleasant experience. Yes, it is intended by God to lead us in some way toward reconciliation with him. That is, divine wrath is a prodding of some sort, designed to lead us to repentance and eventual reconciliation. In that way, we could say that a painful encounter with God's wrath can be instrumentally good for us. Still, the experience itself of being on the receiving end of God's wrathful actions is an unpleasant one. God's act of wrath will be a prodding, but it will be an uncomfortable prodding. My task now is to narrow down further the sort of uncomfortable prodding involved in acts of divine wrath.

As a general point, we humans can be prodded to turn to God by a wide variety of factors. We might experience emotions associated with loneliness, shame, or meaninglessness. Christians sometimes testify that such emotions led them to seek out God and whether God might indeed be the remedy to their distress. We also sometimes find ourselves with desires: to give to those in need, to stand up for those on the margins, to discover whether there is a reason why we are here, and so on. Christians sometimes tell of realizing that the Holy Spirit was kindling in them a desire for God, even before they knew God as Lord and Savior.

Experiences can also move us toward a relationship with God because they affect our intellect. Inevitably, this effect comes in the form of our recognition of some truth. At times this recognition is a matter of seeing something familiar but seeing it in a new way. Jesus' parables show how our intellect can be profoundly affected by common stories. We come to see a lesson for us in the parable of the prodigal son or the good Samaritan. We suddenly see a principle to be learned; we see the moral of the story. We see ourselves in the story—sometimes liking and sometimes not liking what we see. We see others in a new way as well.

These recognitions of some truth can cause us to make changes. We may reconsider our plans, reevaluate our commitments, rethink our priorities. In line with God's aim of drawing us to himself, these kinds of changes in our perspective will hopefully lead us to full repentance, where we move decisively from our sinful ways and to a life of Christian discipleship.

Sometimes our discovery of a new truth will come as welcome news. For example, God may help us to see that we are loved by him unconditionally. This new perspective will be one of relief. That is, we will feel encouraged, we will feel liberated, as God shows us this truth about him and about ourselves.

But, alas, the new truths that God helps us discover will not always be cheerful. The truths associated with God's wrath are not of the cheerful variety. Should we now say that divine wrath is linked to showing us uncomfortable truths? Well, there is some insight to this suggestion. But not all unpleasant truths will be associated with divine wrath. For example, God may help us understand the extent of others' suffering, and this truth may be downright depressing. But our experience of coming to this new understanding would not be one of divine wrath directed toward us. When God pressed on Moses the truth about the Hebrew people's suffering in Egypt, surely this was a painful truth to hear. But Moses was not experiencing God's wrath toward him at that moment.

We get closer to isolating examples of divine wrath when we narrow down the category of painful truths to those that specifically concern us. Painful truths about ourselves are not ones we can simply lament, as when we lament the plight of those who suffered under Hitler or Stalin. When God's wrath is directed toward us, there is some uncomfortable truth that concerns us in some way, something we are expected to do to redress the situation. Even so, in making this point I have still not narrowed things down far enough to describe the core of acting in wrath. A painful truth that specifically concerns us is still not always an expression of divine wrath. God's initial command to Jonah to preach to the Ninevites was a very uncomfortable truth. It did specifically involve Jonah in some way. Yet, it was not itself an expression of God's wrath directed toward Jonah. We must continue to narrow down the category of uncomfortable truths God can reveal to us if we are to arrive at distinctive instances of divine wrath.

The context in Scripture of God's wrath toward people seemingly always has to do with the state of their relationships with others. Specifically, God's wrath seems to arise from the way people have treated someone else. Oftentimes this someone is God. For example, God declares in Jeremiah 7:18: "They pour out drink offerings to other gods to arouse my anger." At other times the someone is other people. For example, God declares in Exodus 22:22 that his anger toward the Hebrew people will be aroused if they "take advantage of the widow or the fatherless." In short, for those on the receiving end of God's wrath, there is some problem with the way that they have treated others, either God or those in the created order.

This moral failing neither is done out of ignorance, nor is it an innocent mistake. It is a willful mistreatment in some way of others. This truth about ourselves—the truth about the morally defective way we have related to others—is the kind of truth that is arousing God's wrath. Again, God's original message to Jonah (to preach to the Ninevites) was not an instance of God's wrath toward Jonah, even though it was a very uncomfortable truth with which Jonah had to contend. However, once Jonah was given this responsibility to preach to the Ninevites, his subsequent running in the other direction was a failure to take responsibility for them. Accordingly, Jonah did at that point open himself up to a potential outpouring of divine wrath.

I am narrowing in now on a working definition of what God's wrath involves. From chapter one, divine wrath is an intentional pattern of action from God, directed toward some individual or group of individuals, and intended for the purpose of some divine goal. From chapters two through four, this goal will be a benevolent one, intended to further people's long-term flourishing. Adding now the

discussion points of this current chapter, I arrive at the following definition of divine wrath. Our experience of God's wrath toward us is
God pressing on us the truth about ourselves.

Pressing on someone the truth about himself is a particular kind
of action. This action can be done in a variety of ways, but there is
nothing unusual about that. A teacher can command a class of students to pay attention by clearing her throat loudly. We can ask a
friend about a stranger in the room by looking the friend in the eye,
raising our eyebrows, and tilting our head in the direction of the
stranger. Whatever the form these speech acts take, commanding
others to pay attention and inquiring about a stranger are kinds of
actions that people can perform. They are basic descriptions of the
actions we all sometimes perform. Likewise, pressing on a person the
truth about himself is a basic description of a kind of action. This is
at the very core of what God is doing when he acts in wrath.

I have already indicated that the kinds of truths about ourselves
at issue here are truths about how we have acted sinfully toward
others. For example, they are truths about how we have mistreated
others, or taken advantage of the powerless, or ignored the pleas of
the poor, or dishonored God, or usurped God's authority in some
manner, and so on. Thus they are truths about our moral failings.
These are not merely truths that God brings to our attention, as he
brought to Jonah's attention that he has been called to preach to the
Ninevites. Rather, these are truths with which God confronts us.
They are truths about ourselves to which we must face up, if we are
to come to full repentance.

Typically, we humans do not react well to suggestions that we have
moral flaws of which we need to repent. Humans typically will resist,
in a variety of ways, uncomfortable truths about themselves. As God
seeks to reveal these kinds of truths to people, God will typically
need to commit to a pattern of action. This continued pattern of

action is what I am referring to by saying that God will *press* on us truths about ourselves.

TRUTH AND PERFECTED RELATIONSHIPS

The reason God would persist in pressing the truth on us is that we must at some point own up to these truths, if we are to be fully and finally reconciled to God. One hallmark of perfected relationships, which the redeemed in heaven all enjoy, is that they are based on truth. Suppose Fred were to cause Sue genuine hurt by some unkind remark he made. Suppose he then offered the somewhat flippant apology: "Oh, sorry if I offended you in some way." Imagine if Sue's response were, "That's okay, it was nothing."

The problem is that it wasn't nothing. Fred genuinely caused hurt. What kind of relationship would they be capable of having after that? It certainly wouldn't be one of genuine honesty and integrity. In order for them to have that kind of relationship moving forward, Fred needs to own up to exactly what he did—and then ask forgiveness for it. He can only do this if he recognizes the truth about how his unkind action truly affected Sue.

Similar considerations reveal one of the reasons why all people must at some point offer Christ's passion up to God as atonement for their own sins. Only in the cross do we see the complete picture of the effects of our sins: jealousy, hubris, cowardice, and all the other sinful traits that could lead humans to think it a good idea to kill the one human life that was lived on earth in moral perfection. These are sins we all have, and this is where they lead. It is only in the cross that we see the full truth of what we have done to God. We also see the full truth of what God has done for us. So there is a sense in which God's invitation to respond to the cross is an invitation to respond to the truth of what our relationship with God has been. (It is also of course an invitation to respond to God's plan to repair that relationship.)

Perhaps for some people God may need to press on them the truth of something positive about them. Those who suffered childhood abuse may have a difficult time ever believing that they have real value and that God delights in them. States of depression can also affect our thinking on such matters. In these cases God may repeatedly need to find ways to help people realize the truth that they are valued and loved. But for many of us, it is the uncomfortable truths about our moral shortcomings that we are especially prone to resist. These are the truths about ourselves that God will need to press on us. Such truths must be recognized by us. We will need to own up to them (and then ask God to forgive us and change us), if a full reconciliation with God based on truth is ever to be achieved.

I noted earlier that divine wrath in the Old Testament is primarily directed toward Israel. In the sequence of things, God's wrath toward other nations is very much subsequent to his outpouring of wrath on his own chosen people. Indeed, it comes as something as a surprise in the book of Jeremiah when God's wrath turns to all the other nations surrounding Judah. The first half of the book of Jeremiah outlines the ways in which Judah has rejected God, resulting in God's outpouring of wrath toward his people. The book of Jeremiah takes a seemingly unexpected turn when he then directs Jeremiah: "Take from my hand this cup filled with the wine of my wrath and make all the nations to whom I send you drink it" (Jeremiah 25:15). The reader then remembers that God's original calling of Jeremiah was indeed to be a "prophet to the nations" (Jeremiah 1:5).

The reasons for God's wrath toward the other nations no doubt included their failure to live up to basic standards of justice. God is said to have charges, or indictments, to bring against the nations, and his judgment is against the wicked, or guilty (Jeremiah 25:31). Still, the nations have not received nearly the light that Israel has received. God had so much hope for Israel, and he had given them so many more resources of divine protection and blessing. Accordingly, more was expected of them. When Israel stubbornly rejected God, there were a great many unhappy truths about themselves that God could press on them. It makes sense that they would bear the brunt of God's wrath. First and foremost in the Old Testament narrative, God presses on the Israelites the truth about themselves—with these acts associated with divine wrath applied only subsequently to other nations.

Whether directed toward Israel or toward other nations, God's wrath in the Bible is again always a *response* to some spiritual sin, some moral failing, some truth about people that they themselves will not admit to. Turning to the New Testament, Jesus' own expressions of anger follow this same pattern. His cleansing of the temple (Mark 11:15-18) points to the people's failure to honor God appropriately. It also underscores the failure of Israel's leaders to guide the people in a way that is true to God's intentions.

Other examples, by now familiar, of Jesus' anger within the New Testament inevitably draw attention to some failure in how people have related to God and/or to the people around them. Jesus becomes indignant when his disciples attempt to prevent children from coming to him (Mark 10:14). He later warns that "If anyone causes one of these little ones—those who believe in me—to stumble, it would be better for them to have a large millstone hung around their neck and to be drowned in the depths of the sea" (Matthew 18:6). Similarly, when Jesus comes on a man with a shriveled hand, he is aware of Pharisees watching, disapprovingly, to see whether he will heal on the Sabbath. As Jesus heals the man, he "looked around at them in anger . . . , deeply distressed at their stubborn hearts" (Mark 3:5). Jesus' concern for the young and the sick of course continues the long biblical theme of God's concern for widows, orphans, and in general anyone on the margins. God's anger toward people becomes an indicator that they are failing the people around them, particularly the vulnerable, whom God has called them especially to support.

God's wrath thus serves as a kind of marker of certain truths about people: truths about their failure to love God and others, truths about their selfishness, truths about their indifference to the plight of their neighbor, and so on. To have God's anger poured out on us is to be accused of some spiritual sin, some moral failing. God's act of wrath is God's act of pressing on us some such uncomfortable truth about who we really are. It is a way of God saying, "*This* is the fact about yourself you must repent of!" There are again a great many ways God may seek to communicate this truth to us, some ways more pleasant than others. Acts of wrath are God's last resort. Still, if God cannot entice and attract us to acknowledge some truth about ourselves, he will press this truth on us by means of actions we associate with his wrath.

Many of the truths about ourselves are inevitably tied up with truths about God. From the Christian perspective, humans have been created by God, are sustained by God, and are called to particular vocational work in which their spiritual gifts (also given by God) can be effectively released. Accordingly, many of the difficult truths about ourselves will involve facing up to the ways we have failed in the past to use the resources God has given us. These difficult truths will also involve the need to set aside undue pride and acknowledge our utter dependence on God's provision and guidance moving forward.

Thus the truths God helps us recognize about our own moral and spiritual standing will be truths that involve our standing in relation to God. Coming to terms with who we are inevitably includes coming to terms with who God is. The biblical descriptions of God's wrath are not only linked with truths the people must acknowledge about themselves; they are also linked with truths the people must recognize about God.

The book of Ezekiel is especially clear on this point. The book is filled from beginning to end with pronouncements of God's judgment.

Themes of divine anger and wrath dominate much of the narrative throughout the book. Interestingly, there is a key phrase that almost inevitably follows God's declarations of wrathful judgment. Specifically, the phrase is "Then they will know that I am the LORD." Ezekiel 25:17 is representative: "I will carry out great vengeance on them and punish them in my wrath. Then they will know that I am the LORD, when I take vengeance on them."

What exactly were the people in the book of Ezekiel failing to recognize about God? In prefacing his message to the Israelites through the priest Ezekiel, God states that he is sending Ezekiel "to a rebellious nation that has rebelled against me; they and their ancestors have been in revolt against me to this very day" (Ezekiel 2:3). This theme of rebellion is of course a dominant one throughout the Christian Scriptures. The simplest way of putting the human problem is that humans can prioritize themselves over God. They can ignore the instructions God has given them. They can make their own plans without consulting God. They can declare that certain outcomes are good ones, whether or not God shares this view. They can confront obstacles with a staunch independence. They can respond to failures by persisting in self-sufficient strategies or by creating their own gods from whom to seek "help." In short, humans can succumb to hubris, or undue pride. Or we might put the point in terms of idolatry: humans can assume a role for themselves that only God should play.

God's acts of wrath are a way of pressing the point that humans cannot flourish in any way other than by complete dependence on him. Ezekiel is again so clear on this point. His favorite title for God is "sovereign LORD," repeated about two hundred times in his book. "LORD" (printed in most English Bibles in capital letters) represents the Hebrew *Yahweh*, which means "I am who I am" or "I will be what I will be." This term expresses the mystery, sovereignty, and authority of God over created beings, and it is revealed to Moses in the story about the burning bush (Exodus 3:2-12). Ezekiel's great concern—indeed, God's great concern—is that people should acknowledge, live by, and benefit from God's authority over their lives. This is the only way any human can flourish in the long run, and so God is desperate that people should "know that I am the Lord" when "I punish them in my wrath." (The other nations must also honor God's sovereignty, which involves honoring God's people. Otherwise, they are liable to wrath and to being destabilized; see Jeremiah 46–51.)

Acknowledging truths about ourselves inevitably involves acknowledging truths about God. We are not self-sufficient, but God is. We are not wise enough to know the paths we should take, but God is. We do not have the power to overcome every obstacle, but God does. We have not always loved the people around us, but God has. The Bible describes Adam and Eve as choosing to chart their own course toward the good life, in contravention to God's instructions about how the good life is actually attained. From that initial sin, humans have continued to repeat this same pattern of thinking of themselves as playing roles that God alone can play. (Thus the continual biblical warning against idolatry.) So when God is pressing on us truths about our shortcomings on these matters, he is also leading us to acknowledge that he alone is LORD.

MOVING FORWARD

God's wrath, once again, is God's last resort. The Old Testament record of the Israelites includes their stubborn refusal to heed repeated warnings that they must rely on God and live by his instructions to love him and love one another if their lives are to go well for them in the long run. But God's people haven't genuinely acknowledged the truth about how they have treated God and others. Now God must press on them, firmly, these truths about themselves.

In the face of such stubborn resistance, it would be ineffective for the Israelites simply to be told once again about their relationship with God. God must press on them firmly, uncompromisingly, harshly the truth about themselves in relation to God. God must show them the state of their relationship with him. This pattern of pressing on people uncomfortable truths about themselves is God acting in wrath, or pouring out his wrath on them. The way God is seen in Scripture as pressing the truth on people, as well as the reason God really must press the truth on us as a corrective to sin, will be further explored in the next chapter.

6

TRUTH AS GOD'S RESPONSE
TO SIN AND SELF-DECEPTION

In the previous chapter I outlined a way of understanding what God is doing when he acts in wrath. He is pressing on people uncomfortable truths about themselves, inevitably including truths about how they relate to and have responded to God. I want to begin this chapter by looking at the general way God presses on people the truth about themselves before moving on to discuss why this pressing of the truth must be at the core of God's response to human sin.

THE GENERAL WAY GOD PRESSES THE TRUTH IN WRATH

It is worth emphasizing once again that divine wrath is only one divine response to human sin. It is only one way for God to help people face up to difficult truths about themselves. My concern in this book is for those particular times when God's actions of holding the truth in front of us are describable in terms of God acting in wrath. At such times, the way God presses on people the truth about themselves and their relationship with God is by showing them what life is like when God's blessing and protection is absent. If people are choosing to reject God's provision and guidance, then God offers people a foretaste of what life apart from him is truly like.

Looking through Scripture, very often God does this simply by removing his blessing and protection. For the Israelites the result is that they become vulnerable to disease, hunger, and military defeats:

"I will not look on you with pity or spare you. A third of your people will die of the plague or perish by famine inside you; a third will fall by the sword outside your walls; and a third I will scatter to the winds and pursue with drawn sword" (Ezekiel 5:11-12). Similar language is used a chapter later, linked to God pouring out his wrath: "One who is far away will die of the plague, and one who is near will fall by the sword, and anyone who survives and is spared will die of famine. So will I pour out my wrath on them" (Ezekiel 6:12). God's wrath thus seems connected here with God lifting his protective hand and allowing things to take their course. Indeed, there are references throughout Ezekiel to God withdrawing his favor from Israel, such as "the glory of the LORD departed from over the threshold of the temple" (Ezekiel 10:18).

Throughout the Bible particular phrases are often used to convey this idea of God withdrawing from people, as an act associated with wrath. One such phrase is God hiding his face from people. For example, in Deuteronomy 31 God warns of the time in which Israel will forsake him, declaring, "In that day I will become angry with them and forsake them; I will hide my face from them, and they will be destroyed. Many disasters and calamities will come on them" (Deuteronomy 31:17). In Psalm 27 we find the psalmist pleading, "Do not hide your face from me, do not turn your servant away in anger" (Psalm 27:9). Other examples include Deuteronomy 32:20-22; Psalms 88:14; 102:2; Isaiah 54:8; 57:17; 64:5-7. This phrase of course conveys the opposite idea of the priestly blessing: "the LORD make his face shine on you" (Numbers 6:25).

Another common phrase is God handing over or giving over people. The psalmist declares that "the LORD was angry with his people and abhorred his inheritance. He gave them into the hands of the nations, and their foes ruled over them" (Psalm 106:40-41). Similarly, "He gave his people over to the sword; he was furious with his inheritance" (Psalm 78:62). (God's inheritance in these contexts refers to his people Israel, as is clear in such places as Psalm 78:71 and Deuteronomy 9:29.) We read God's declaration in Jeremiah 12:7: "I will give the one I love into the hands of her enemies." The book of Judges records that "in his anger against Israel the LORD gave them into the hands of raiders who plundered them" (Judges 2:14).

Similar phrases throughout Scripture express the same general idea. We read that, when the Israelites forsook God, "he became angry with them. He sold them into the hands of the Philistines and the Ammonites" (Judges 10:7-8). This description of selling people over in wrath is repeated in such places as Judges 3:8 and 1 Samuel 12:9. Sometimes the wording follows Nehemiah 9:27 in stating that God "delivered them into the hands of their enemies." Judges 13:1 and 2 Chronicles 28:5 likewise use this language of being delivered into some calamity.

All these phrases seem to carry the idea of God withdrawing protection or blessing and allowing disaster of some kind to befall people. The people are given over to some threat, often the threat of a hostile nation. Interestingly, Isaiah 64:7 laments that God has "given us over to our sins." Paul picks up this theme in the New Testament of being given over to sin. He writes of God giving people over to their "sinful desires" (Romans 1:24, 26) and "to a depraved mind" (Romans 1:28). Paul's reprimand of the church in Corinth is that they have not in turn followed this practice; they have failed to hand over an unrepentant member "to Satan" (1 Corinthians 5:5).

The common theme in this language of giving over is that God withdraws from people. In a clear sense, he gives them what they want. He allows them to fulfill their existing desires. If his people are determined to reject God and live according to their own devices, then they will experience what life is like when God is not supporting them. They will learn about their own limitations and vulnerabilities. They will learn just how significant God's provisions really are, which they had failed to appreciate and had even spurned. God's actions are like that of a caring but exasperated parent who has tried everything to help correct a son or daughter's behavior. Eventually, the parent may withdraw all support from the child, as a final and extreme measure of prodding the child to come to his or her senses.

I earlier noted that God very often presses the truth on people simply by removing his blessing and protection. Sometimes, however, the biblical language associated with divine wrath is difficult to account for merely with the idea of God withdrawing. God's actions in wrath at times seem to have a more proactive component. God is sometimes said to raise up or bring up agents to carry out his wrath. For example, in 2 Chronicles 36:17 we read of Israel's plight: "He brought up against them the king of the Babylonians, who killed their young men with the sword in the sanctuary." Later on, Babylon does not escape God's wrath, described again in seemingly proactive terms: "I set a trap for you, Babylon, and you were caught before you knew it; you were found and captured because you opposed the LORD" (Jeremiah 50:24). Yes, Babylon has been an agent of God's wrath against Israel, but "how the LORD our God has taken vengeance, vengeance for his temple" (Jeremiah 50:28). Therefore, "The LORD has stirred up the kings of the Medes, because his purpose is to destroy Babylon" (Jeremiah 51:11).

Conceivably, such references to the seemingly proactive nature of God's wrath might all be interpreted as simply God withdrawing protection. But it seems more natural to read such passages as God actively pressing the issue, doing more than merely withdrawing. Either way, though, the main point still remains. God is showing people what life apart from his protective support looks like. He is pressing on them the truth about themselves. The people have sought to go their own way and spurned a relationship of dependence on God.

They are getting a taste of what that life is like. They are profoundly overoptimistic about their own abilities. They are under the illusion that they do not need God, that they can live well if left to their own devices. God has little choice at this point but to press the truth, no matter how painful to them, that he alone is Lord and that they cannot flourish in the long run without relating to him as such.

BLINDNESS TO THE TRUTH ABOUT OUR LIFE WITH GOD

In the rest of this chapter I want to say more about why it is so vital for God to press truth on people. I have already discussed how an eternal, perfected relationship with God must be built on truth. We must see and acknowledge the truth about who we are, what we've done to God, and what God has done for us in Christ. Only *then* can our relationships with God be genuinely honest and open. I have also noted how the acts we associate with God's wrath are prompts for us to acknowledge sinful truths about ourselves and to repent of them. (Indeed, God abandons his wrathful pursuits when repentance occurs.)

In the following two sections I want to discuss the extent to which humans can be blind to and can actively resist uncomfortable truths about themselves. This of course is the *reason* God must persist in pressing on people these uncomfortable truths, sometimes taking drastic actions associated with wrath. Perhaps the best way into this discussion is to consider why someone might be blind even to truths about heaven. I am ultimately concerned with the way people may be blinded to the truth about themselves—and to how a good life is possible only through radical obedience to God. But if a person cannot even see heaven as a good place, it will be impossible for that person to see obedience to God as a good thing. Thus a discussion of heaven is instructive about how a person can be blind to the truth that a life of dependence on God is key to the good life.

The Christian description of heaven is one of ultimate flourishing for humans. The redeemed in heaven enjoy experiences of boundless love, peace, and joy. The biblical imagery of heaven includes "springs of living water," cities "of pure gold," a place where God "will wipe every tear" from our eyes (Revelation 7:17; 21:4, 18). So why would any person refuse God's invitation to eternal life with him in heaven?

It would be one thing to suggest that a person might not accept God's invitation to an eternal relationship with him due to ignorance of the invitation. Some people never hear the gospel message in their earthly lives or hear only a distorted version of the person and work of Jesus. However, I want to follow John Wesley (and others) in reasoning that, in the end, only a *willful rejection* of God will keep a person from final reconciliation with God in heaven. C. S. Lewis affirmed this perspective with the memorable expression that "the doors of hell are locked on the inside."[1] In other words, people who are separated from God are themselves refusing to be reconciled to him.

The question again arises: Why would a person not want to be reconciled to God, given that our reconciliation with God involves the unparalleled good news of heaven for us? The short answer is that the good news of life with God in heaven will not seem like *good* news to everyone. Yes, the biblical imagery of heaven is appropriate for those who have made Jesus Lord and are following him. But the delights of heaven cannot be enjoyed by just anyone. They can only be enjoyed by those with a certain moral disposition.

The Christian view of human flourishing is *not* that it consists fundamentally in external pleasures: enjoying fine food, music, art, scenery, and so forth. Instead, the Christian view is that our ultimate flourishing is achieved when our relationships—with God and with

---

[1]C. S. Lewis, *The Problem of Pain* (New York: HarperCollins, 1996), 131.

others—are perfected in love. After all, external things such as food, scenery, and so forth will not be enjoyed by someone who is in the midst of loneliness or conflict. (As Proverbs 17:1 indicates, "Better a dry crust of bread with peace and quiet than a house full of feasting, with strife.")

Humans are created in the image of a relational God, and our ultimate flourishing is achieved when we engage in relationships mirroring the loving interdependence of the Trinity. The rewards of heaven are simply the inherent joys of relating to God and to others within perfected relationships. I don't want to deny that God may give the redeemed in heaven beautiful scenes to enjoy or perhaps elegant banquets to share. But I think Christians must hold fast in affirming that these external objects are not the *source* of our enjoyment. God is that source, and we enjoy God by relating positively to him and to others in whom his Spirit dwells, even as our shared ventures may include activities such as viewing beautiful scenery.

As discussed in chapter two, the loving interdependence of perfected relationships (as seen within the Trinity) involves a pouring out of oneself for others. To a person fully committed to serving God and others in love, the community of perfected relationships in heaven will be the best news imaginable. But to someone who pursues self-interest over against benevolence, the invitation to heaven will not be good news. After all, the invitation to participate in the heavenly community is the invitation to serve, following Christ's example.

In and of itself, self-interest is not a bad thing. We would not live very long if we did not pursue water, food, and shelter for ourselves. The pleasures of viewing art, music, movies, sporting events, and so forth do provide a certain enjoyment. But the Christian message is that these enjoyments will have diminishing returns, unless they are enjoyed with others and ultimately with God. Again, our relationships will be the key to whether we flourish in the long run. But by prioritizing our own interests above others over and over again, we can become blind to the clear truth of where our well-being ultimately lies.

Every Christmas season, we can view a very clear illustration of how a person can become utterly blind to where his or her well-being actually lies. The movie *It's a Wonderful Life* serves as a great illustration of how selfish pursuits ultimately lead to our own self-destruction. In this classic movie, Mr. Potter is the richest man in town, determined to increase his own wealth by keeping others poor and powerless. By the end of the movie, he is alone, isolated, un-loved, and avoided by everyone in town. Still, he tenaciously clings to the hope of bringing down the one person who won't grovel beneath him: Jimmy Stewart's character, George Bailey. He steals from George Bailey, anticipating the pleasure of seeing his nemesis finally ruined.

But of course what happens is that the town rallies to George Bailey's defense. George has spent his life helping the people in town, often at great cost to himself. The people are more than happy to offer their support in George's time of need. At the end of the movie he is proclaimed "the richest man in town." Theologically, we might say that he is living into the great paradox Jesus taught: only when a person loses his life will he find it (Matthew 10:39).

But back to Mr. Potter. We see near the end of the movie that he is utterly miserable. We want to say, "If you'd just *give* of yourself instead of *taking*, you'd start to be happy! You'd start to be more like George Bailey, who has *real* happiness." But Mr. Potter persists in trying to find some pleasure, some sense of gratification, in gaining more for himself at the expense of others. Given the lack of any loving relation-ships in his life, any semblance of pleasure at this point is pretty non-existent. But because of his settled moral character from a lifetime of selfishness, the strategy of subjugating others still seems attractive to

him. It seems the best strategy for the good life, and the goal of benevolence still seems like the strategy of suckers and chumps.

While Mr. Potter's attitude is an extreme one, surely we can all recognize this same tendency toward stinginess and selfishness at times
in ourselves and in others we have met in life. The path of service,
compassion, and forgiveness can sometimes seem so demanding. We
can ask ourselves: Is the way of the cross really the way to fullness of
life? As Christians, we can only affirm that it is. But we need wisdom
to see the truth in Jesus' paradox about losing and gaining our lives.
We need trust in the promises of God. We need encouragement from
others who are trying to follow the path of Christ along with us.

The path of Mr. Potter by the end of the movie has of course become
very narrow. He is constricted on all sides by his misery and his failure
to have any network of healthy relationships. But the path on which
he *began* was all too easy. It was a broad road, as Jesus called it
(Matthew 7:13). Prioritizing self over God, self over others, is hardly
any task at all. It is something we naturally fall into if we do nothing
to resist this pattern.

Our day-to-day decisions of course shape our character. When we
respond to the prompting of the Holy Spirit, who urges us toward love
of God and others, we are conformed more and more to the likeness
of Christ. But when we resist this prompting, prioritizing self over
God and others, we become more and more like, well, Mr. Potter. Our
specific sins might be different from his, but the end result is the same.
From a vantage point of increasing misery, we grasp all the more
desperately for some pleasure from our selfish pursuits. We will fail
to see the opportunity for loving service as good in any way.

THE PATH TO SELF-DECEPTION

A settled moral disposition takes time to develop. No one becomes
Mr. Potter in a day. How do we become blind to large, glaringly

obvious truths (such as the attractiveness of heaven)? By turning our attention away from smaller truths over a period of time. How do we become blind to deep truths about our own moral character? By turning our attention away from smaller, uncomfortable truths about ourselves over a period of time.

If there is one kind of truth that we humans are adept at avoiding, it is the thought that we have been acting in a morally defective way. Facing up to such truths about ourselves is always uncomfortable. Here is what modern psychologists have sadly documented all too well: we humans have devised a staggering array of strategies to avoid uncomfortable truths about ourselves.

As an initial point, we humans can be very selective in the way we think about the evidence for and against our good character. We can find it easy to remember reasons why we should be promoted at work, but more difficult to reflect on the reasons why a colleague should receive the promotion. We can find it easy to remember our past acts of generosity, but more difficult to think of the times we have been stingy. We can find it easy to remember that we have washed the dishes a lot of times in the past few weeks, but more difficult to be impressed by the number of times our spouse may have taken care of the washing up.

Sports fans do this kind of selective remembering all the time. It is fascinating to watch a game such as basketball on television while in a room with fans from both teams. Each group of fans ends up yelling at the referees. Each group sees the fouls that are being committed against the players on their *own* team. Each group sees the traveling violations being committed by the players on the *other* team. Each group ends up yelling at the referees, genuinely convinced that the bulk of the referees' missed calls are going against their own team. The neutral observer naturally wonders how the referees can be working so effectively against both teams!

This kind of selective viewing of evidence occurs constantly in daily life. Philosophers and psychologists have long observed the powerful effects that our desires have on our beliefs. As a general rule, when we desire something to be true, we are much more likely to come to believe that it is true. This tendency affects our evaluation of a referee's performance, our evaluation of our children's athletic potential, our evaluation of which presidential candidate is the most dignified, and so on. Very often, we humans settle on a conclusion we desire to be the case. Then we selectively focus our attention on the evidence that supports our favored conclusion.

All this is especially so when it comes to the deeply personal issue of our own character. It is one thing to admit that our favorite sports team is just not as good as a rival team. But it is a more difficult thing to admit that the personal choices we are making about how to spend our money and to live our lives are morally corrupt. It is much easier to turn our attention away from such uncomfortable thoughts. Every time we selectively consider evidence about ourselves, the contrary evidence we are putting out of mind becomes easier to forget completely. Thus, over time it becomes easier and easier to sincerely believe that our favored picture of ourselves really is the truth of the matter.

When we *are* confronted with contrary evidence, which we are unable to selectively avoid, we humans have another trick. We can find ways to reframe the evidence. Here, psychological studies confirm the extraordinary lengths to which we humans can go to avoid uncomfortable truths about ourselves. We can remind ourselves (and others) that everyone has faults. We can tell ourselves that our behavior is not among the really serious sins and that it is not really hurting anyone. We can explain our transgressions as temporary and uncharacteristic lapses, not representative of who we truly are.

We humans are good at minimizing or even sabotaging the efforts of friends, so that our own behavior looks good by comparison. We can inhibit our own performances—for instance, by consuming alcohol—so that we have a ready-made excuse should we commit some indiscretion. In some instances we can even embrace the diagnosis of a mental or physical illness because the conclusion "I'm unwell" is more comfortable than the conclusion "I'm willfully engaged in unacceptable behavior." (Of course in other instances we may indeed be unwell in some way, and here a false accusation of willful sin is emphatically *not* what helps lead us to the truth about ourselves. I am speaking only of those particular contexts in which humans are actively seeking to avoid owning up to existing facts about their own moral character.)

If these reframing strategies fail, there is always the option simply to pretend to have the moral character that sits well with our conscience. We can put on a brave face to others, communicating to them that all is well. Interestingly, as modern psychology has again documented, we humans are remarkably good at (very quickly) coming to believe that we possess the moral character we were initially only pretending to have.

This is by no means a complete list of all the ways humans can willfully choose to avoid uncomfortable truths about themselves. But it hopefully gives some indication of the complex task the Holy Spirit may need to undertake in helping a person face up to the truth that "No, I'm not the person I've been trying to picture myself as being." All the little ways we avoid uncomfortable truths in day-to-day life will need to be countered by persisting messages from the Holy Spirit regarding the true state of our relationships with God and with others. Once again, only when we face up to the whole truth about ourselves can we then participate in relationships of honesty and integrity, such as the redeemed in heaven enjoy with God and with one another.

To sum up some of the points of the past two sections, only a person's free, willful rejection of God will prevent full and final reconciliation with God. Given the incredibly good news of what this final reconciliation involves (eternal joy in heaven), the only way a person could willfully reject this good news is that it does not seem to a person that it is good news. The offer of heaven is, from the Christian perspective, an offer to love and serve God and others. But to a person stubbornly clinging to selfish pursuits as the key to (ever elusive) happiness, this offer is decidedly unattractive. A person can become blinded to the truth about his own well-being through a continued refusal to acknowledge that there is anything wrong or unattractive about his ongoing pattern of selfish desires and action.

The key to combating this pathway to self-deception is for someone to press on us the truth about the state of our moral character. This is precisely what God is doing when he acts toward us in a way we associate with wrath. Yes, the biblical language of divine wrath can seem quite harsh. But God must at times be forceful and uncompromising in pressing on us the truth about ourselves, given how creative and persistent we humans can be in avoiding these uncomfortable truths. So there is a crucial sense in which God pressing on us the truth about ourselves is God's fundamental response to the cluster of related human conditions: sin, self-deception, and spiritual blindness.

Admittedly, the biblical narrative tends to emphasize the way humans can suppress the truth about *God*. For instance, the Gospel of John records Jesus remarking that "whoever rejects the Son will not see life, for God's wrath remains on them" (John 3:36). When the apostle Paul talks about the wicked who "suppress the truth," the context is his discussion of "what may be known about God" (Romans 1:18-19). But of course the question then becomes why we would suppress the truth about God. The answer involves the implications God's existence and commands would have for us: our preferred choices, lifestyle, and so forth. When God works to counter our rejection of the truth, it really is the truth about ourselves—and how we want to position ourselves in relation to God—that will be his focus. (Interestingly, Paul goes on to remark: "For those *who are self-seeking* and who reject the truth and follow evil, there will be wrath and anger" in Romans 2:8.)

THE SIGNIFICANCE OF UNFORGIVENESS AND JUDGMENT OF OTHERS

Understanding the importance of owning up to the truth about ourselves helps in making sense of some surprisingly stark warnings that Jesus gave. In particular, two cautions really do stand out in Jesus' teachings to his followers: his caution against (1) unforgiveness and (2) judging others. As recorded in Matthew 6, Jesus instructs his disciples how to pray (the Lord's Prayer) as part of his Sermon on the Mount. After concluding this prayer, Jesus zeroes in on one particular aspect of the prayer: forgiveness. He warns his followers that "if you do not forgive others their sins, your Father will not forgive your sins" (Matthew 6:15).

Continuing with the Sermon on the Mount, Jesus soon comes to the matter of judging others. He again issues a striking word of warning: "Do not judge, or you too will be judged. For in the same way you judge others, you will be judged, and with the measure you use, it will be measured to you" (Matthew 7:1-2). As with Jesus' statement about unforgiveness, there seems to be a condition about judging others that is attached to God's forgiveness of us. This may initially strike us as odd, given the way Jesus modeled unconditional love for us and sought at all costs to draw us to himself.

What is so significant about the failure to forgive and about the practice of judging others? To identify them as conditions for God's forgiveness is to assign them a hugely significant role. These conditions may initially strike us as puzzling. But the crucial role of owning up to the truth about ourselves helps to make sense of why these conditions are in place.

Consider a situation in which we fail to forgive someone else, particularly when we are also asking God to forgive our own failings. The

stance we are implicitly taking is this: the other person has committed
a level of offense that I haven't committed. My offense can reasonably
be forgiven, but his offense is really beyond the pale.

But this stance is a refusal to own up to the fact that we are all in
the same boat. We all have committed offenses that we are powerless
to make right. The truth from God is that all people, when they turn
to God, can come to participate in the community of perfected relationships in heaven. Those people who have committed offenses
against us may therefore be among the people in heaven we are called
to serve in love. A refusal to forgive others ends up being a rejection
of the truth about who we are and about how our ultimate flourishing
(through benevolence) can singularly be achieved.

Jesus again reserves some of his harshest language for those who
resist forgiving others. In his parable of the king who settles accounts
(Matthew 18:23-35), the king cancels a servant's debt, only to find out
later that this servant has failed to be similarly merciful to a fellow
servant who was in debt to the servant. The king confronts the servant
with severe language, "You wicked servant" (Matthew 18:32). Then, "in
anger," the king "handed him over to the jailers to be tortured, until he
should pay back all he owed" (Matthew 18:34). Jesus concludes with the
warning, "This is how my heavenly Father will treat each of you unless
you forgive your brother or sister from your heart" (Matthew 18:35).

This is a harrowing portrait Jesus gives us of a spiritual truth. But
it is once again no wonder that Jesus would give such a stark warning
about the dangers of refusing to forgive others. Unforgiveness pre-
vents us from acknowledging and repenting of vital truths about ourselves. Without owning up to these truths and placing them before
God, we end up not taking advantage of God's offer to forgive all the
things we place before him. Yes, the acts of prompting to repentance
are dire—but they still pale in comparison to the eternally dire consequences of not owning up to the truth about ourselves.

Turning to the matter of judging others, I am not of course talking about "judging" another person's behavior. Part of Christian accountability is candidly drawing attention to one another's behavior when it violates God's instructions about how he wants us to live together. The danger of judgmentalism arises when we presume to pass judgment on the motivations and moral character that lie behind another person's actions. As 1 Samuel 16:7 reminds us, "People look at the outward appearance, but the LORD looks at the heart." God alone can see how others have responded internally to the difficulties and to the grace they have been given.

When we judge other people's moral character, their spiritual state, we again implicitly take a kind of stance. We presume that we do not have the kinds of character flaws that they do. Whatever our flaws are, at least they are not at the level of those flaws.

But once again, this stance amounts to a refusal to acknowledge vital truths about ourselves and about the life of flourishing to which God invites us. It is no wonder that Jesus would indicate that God's judgment of us is conditioned by our judgment of others.

With the words "in the same way you judge others, you will be judged," Jesus is seemingly offering a message along the following lines: "If you *really* think that you don't have the kind of flaw you're pointing out in someone else, then chances are you are blind to this fact about yourself. God will need to press this truth on you, and you will need to acknowledge and repent of it, if full and final reconciliation with God is to occur." Ezekiel 7:27 is interesting to consider in this regard: "I will deal with them according to their conduct, and by their own standards I will judge them."

MOVING FORWARD

In this chapter I have discussed the way God presses the truth on people when he acts in wrath. In short, he gives them a taste of the disastrous life that awaits any person who is truly separated from God's life-giving presence and blessing. I have discussed some of the ways people can blind themselves to the truth about how their ultimate well-being is achieved. This pattern of self-deceptive practices inevitably involves refusing to acknowledge truths about one's own moral flaws. Specifically, these flaws involve embracing selfishness over benevolence. As happiness proves more and more elusive, a person may still persist in grasping for some kind of pleasure through increasingly self-centered pursuits. The end result may be self-inflicted blindness to the otherwise obvious fact that God's invitation to loving fellowship is good for us.

To combat this path toward self-destruction, God must move people to own up to the truth about themselves. God's pressing on us of the truth about ourselves is God's response to people's patterns of self-deception. It is God addressing the root of what keeps people from recognizing his offer of love as *good* for them.

I anticipate the objection that divine wrath must somehow be more than this. I have noted that a taste of life apart from God's protection and blessing can be painful; and I have acknowledged that the biblical language describing God's wrath can be harsh. But perhaps one might think that I have been too civil about all this. Perhaps it is an understatement to say that the biblical language is harsh. It can also be described as alarming, chilling, something of unparalleled dread. By comparison, the idea of God merely calling our attention to the truth about ourselves may seem so minimal, so watered down by comparison. In the following chapter I want to show that nothing could be further from the truth.

7

THE PAIN OF TRUTH AS OUR GREATEST PAIN

In this chapter I consider the objection that divine wrath surely must refer to something more, something stronger, than God merely conveying truths of some kind to us. My general response is that the well-known phrase "the truth hurts" is far more profound than we might initially imagine. There actually is no sharper weapon that God could wield against us humans than the truth about ourselves.

The Unique Discomfort of Being Confronted with the Truth

There are various kinds of pains that humans can experience. Physical pains are one example, and they themselves come in various forms. Stubbing a toe feels different from the pain of arthritis, which feels different from the pain of nausea. Still, they all feel bad. Emotional pains can also vary greatly. The feeling associated with a friend's betrayal is different from the feeling of losing a job, which is different from how it feels to remember childhood abuse. But emotional pains again will all feel bad to us.

Whether we experience trauma to the body or suffer from emotional distress, our pains in life are things with which we humans try to cope. This point is easy to overlook, but it's very significant: *we* try to cope with *them*. We reflect on our pains, we analyze them, and we search for ways in which to minimize their impact on us. In short, we try to distance ourselves from them.

Sometimes it is easy to distance ourselves from our pains. We remind each other that stepping in a hole and breaking an ankle is simply bad luck. The death of a family pet is just one of those things. Getting cancer is one of the vagaries of life. Life in general can be cruel. In this way we can quickly distance ourselves from pains that are no fault of our own. Yes, we may still experience pain of a certain kind. But there remains a sense in which we are rising above our pain and not wallowing, immobilized, in a state of abject misery. Indeed, the apostles Paul (Romans 5:3), Peter (1 Peter 4:13), and James (James 1:2) all remind us that there is a sense in which Christians can even count it joy when they suffer.

It is more difficult to distance ourselves from painful experiences when we know that these experiences are a result of our own missteps. After all, our pain cannot be dismissed as something that unluckily comes to us from the outside. Reflecting on these kinds of pains involves owning up to them. This process of owning up to them carries with it a layer of pain in and of itself. We associate this kind of deep pain with feelings of regret, guilt, and shame.

Nevertheless, it is still possible to achieve some distance between ourselves and our past mistakes. In owning up to our past mistakes, there is a clear sense in which we are confirming that we are not the same person we once were. That is, in lamenting some past deed, we are doing so from the perspective that we now renounce such deeds. We have grown morally in some way.

From our vantage point now, we can therefore distance ourselves from the pain brought on by past failings (that is, the failings of our former selves). We can find a variety of ways to cope with this pain. For instance, we can lean on the understanding shoulders of others, perhaps others who also are recovering from self-destructive lifestyles. Such coping mechanisms are available because, once again, we are able to frame our pain as something *we* are now having to endure.

At least, in the case of self-destructive actions from the past, we are able to frame our pain as something that our current selves are enduring, even while acknowledging that our former selves were responsible for it. Maintaining this kind of distance from our pain allows us to say: "*I* am experiencing something that is not wholly reflective of who *I* really am." The ability to maintain this perspective on our pain is crucial to maintaining an identity that is removed in some way from the pain. With our identity intact, we can again find ways of coping with the outside pain that comes *to us*.

Things are very different when it comes to unacknowledged misdeeds. From the Christian perspective, our unacknowledged misdeeds will already be causing us pain, for they will already be preventing us from enjoying the loving, truthful relationships with God and others through which we can find lasting peace and joy. When someone then attempts to point out my misdeeds, this will feel like someone pouring salt in my wound. "Something is already 'not right' about my life. Why is this person insisting that it's somehow my fault?! Wasn't that the insensitive offense of Job's so-called friends?"

Again, when we humans experience pains and trials, we naturally seek ways of coping with them, which involve distancing ourselves from them. If someone suggests to us that our pain is the result of our own (unacknowledged) moral flaws, then the suggestion will be a deeply painful (and perhaps infuriating) one to us. Moreover, the suggestion also serves as a challenge to the very way we are trying to cope with our pains. That is, the suggestion disrupts our effort to retain a vantage point from which *we* are enduring *them*. The suggestion is that there are not external pains which are occurring to us. *We* are the very problem.

When someone challenges the core picture we have of ourselves, it is uniquely unsettling. The core of our very identity is under attack. Of course, we might acknowledge our moral flaws, repent of them, and then take up the vantage point of one who now knows better. Such a process would allow us to begin to distance ourselves from our pain, and we could then explore ways of coping with it (for example, by apologizing to those we have wronged and being restored to fellowship with them). But in cases of unacknowledged wrongdoing, we cannot come to this vantage point. We still believe we have nothing to confess and repent of. The suggestion to the contrary feels like a cruel attack—again, an attack on our very identity.

As someone repeatedly presses and presses on us this insistence that the problem is us, and as we persist in refusing this conclusion, the arrows of perceived cruelty toward us are relentless. We can get no peace from the onslaught. The reminder that we might be at fault is continually pressed on us; and the reminder is continually unsettling. Again, what is being undercut is our coping mechanism, our attempt to find some vantage point from which to reflect on all this discomfort and find some avenue of relief. Worse still, imagine that someone's way of confronting us is to ensure that we endure calamitous events, which are intended to make us face up to the uncomfortable truths about our own shortcomings. (This of course is what God's acts of wrath commonly amount to, as seen in the biblical narrative. God gives people a foretaste of how life apart from his blessing ultimately descends into disaster.)

In such a case, the pressing on me of some truth about myself really amounts to heaping on levels of hot coals. I am in the midst of external pains as I am given a taste of what my self-destructive actions are leading to. I try to cope with these pains by maintaining an identity over and above these pains. But this coping mechanism is being undercut by the way the external pains challenge the view of myself I am struggling so hard to maintain. This challenge is deeply unsettling, since to acknowledge my shortcomings would be to admit that my real identity is one of moral depravity. In short, I would be in the most pitiable of circumstances.

All this is not to say that God intends our abject misery as his ultimate goal. His ultimate goal remains the benevolent one of prompting us to turn to him in acknowledgment of who we are and who he is. Even when people persist in resisting God's prompting, there is no reason to think that God's benevolent goal changes. Indeed, consistent with the conclusions of chapters two and three, about God's essential benevolence and his revelation that he loves us, there is much reason to insist that God's benevolent goal is steadfast. This remains so, even though the pains of experiencing God's wrath are in a clear sense the sharpest kinds of pain we could experience.

EXPERIENCING GOD'S PROMPTING AS WRATH

I have discussed in this chapter how God's actions of pressing the truth on us serve as a kind of assault on our coping mechanisms. We try to cope with pain and suffering by distancing ourselves from it in some way. Our coping strategy is hindered by the recurring message that the difficulty we're trying to overcome is actually *ourselves*. To make matters worse, the best means God sometimes has of prompting us to face up to the truth is to orchestrate painful external events in our lives (which of course are all the more painful because our coping mechanisms are being undermined).

A further aspect of the discomfort we may feel as God presses the truth on us involves the activity of the Holy Spirit. The Christian Scriptures make reference to God writing his law on the human heart. Inasmuch as people retain some aspect of a moral conscience involving their own shortcomings, even as they strain to resist the truth God is pressing on them, people will be in a state of "dis-ease." That is, they will have some awareness of the truth, even as they continue in their refusal to confront it.

Psychologists sometimes talk about the importance of having an integrated self. We may debate how exactly to characterize all the

aspects of the human person: physical aspects, mental aspects, spiritual aspects. But Christians will agree that one role of the Holy Spirit
is to convict, or "prove the world to be in the wrong about sin"
(John 16:8). It is only reasonable to think that this conviction of sin
will manifest itself in the various aspects of the human person.
Humans of course are so much more than their conscious thoughts.
We can all be deeply affected by unconscious beliefs, nagging feelings,
and so on.

Accordingly, our efforts to ignore God's pressing of the truth on us
will never be wholly successful. Given the Holy Spirit's influence,
some parts of us will always be affected by this truth. Again, we can
debate whether these parts of us are best described as unconscious
beliefs, or frustrated desires, or unpleasant emotions, or something
irreducibly spiritual. But the parts of us that are disquieted by the
influence of the Holy Spirit will always prevent all the parts of us from
being fully integrated. Any attempt to deny the truth about ourselves
will never be wholly successful. The resulting psychological and spiritual state of dis-ease will bring its own kind of misery—which, once
again, we will find all the more difficult to cope with, given that our
coping mechanisms are weakened in the process.

I began this chapter by considering an objection to the explanation
of divine wrath offered in chapter six. The objection is that God
pressing on people the truth about themselves is too mild to account
for the harrowing biblical imagery of divine wrath. My response has
been that, when we are pressed with uncomfortable moral truths
about ourselves that we persist in refusing to accept, we experience a
kind of pain that is unparalleled. It is a painful experience that attacks
our very self-identity and obstructs our ability to cope. Instead of
thinking this kind of pressing of the truth to be mild, we should instead think of it as involving the kind of pain that cuts us to the heart
most deeply. Accordingly, the severe imagery of divine wrath we find

in the Bible actually lines up quite well with the kind of torment experienced as God presses and presses the truth on someone who is stubbornly resisting it.

The lengths to which people go in the Bible to resist truths about themselves is sometimes staggering. It begins with Adam's attempt to deflect blame when God confronts him over his first sin: "The woman you put here with me—she gave me some fruit from the tree, and I ate it" (Genesis 3:12). Even God is not above being blamed as we seek to minimize our own moral failings.

The book of Isaiah is particularly insightful in describing how humans can resist truths about themselves. One of the striking aspects about Isaiah is the extreme disconnect between how the people view themselves and how God sees them. The people pour out complaints against God: "Why have we fasted . . . , and you have not seen it? Why have we humbled ourselves, and you have not noticed?" (Isaiah 58:3). The people are keeping up their end of the bargain, but God is not doing his part. At least, that is the thinking of the people.

But God has a radically different perspective on the spiritual state of the people. He reminds the people that, while fasting, "you do as you please and exploit all your workers" (Isaiah 58:3). Israel's purpose as God's instrument was to be a light to the world: "to loose the chains of injustice and untie the cords of the yoke, to set the oppressed free and break every yoke" (Isaiah 58:6). This has been the act of worship, the fast, to which God has called his people. But the people have failed to live up to this role. And so God asks rhetorically, "Is that what you call a fast, a day acceptable to the LORD?" (Isaiah 58:5).

God here is incredulous at the people's insistence that they themselves are somehow righteous. He declares at one point that they are a people who "call evil good and good evil, who put darkness for light and light for darkness" (Isaiah 5:20). The people emphasize how they are humbling themselves, how they are fasting, how they are really worshiping God. From the people's perspective, whatever the problem is, it's not of their doing. It must be God who is not keeping up his end of the bargain.

Yes, this is an absurd conclusion. But we humans can be driven to such absurd conclusions by how deeply uncomfortable it is to consider that perhaps *we* are the problem. Whatever the difficulty we face, we humans can seek desperately the vantage point that the difficulty we're in is a pain coming to us from the outside that we must suffer through.

This quest to detach ourselves from our pains is again the natural, human way of dealing with them. But when combined with a selfish insistence that we are never the real problem, humans become capable of extreme stubbornness in the face of truths that should be obvious. This helps explain the acute contrast between God's views and the people's views in the book of Isaiah. It helps explain the lengths to which God must sometimes go in pressing on people truths about themselves.

To people who persist in resisting God's truths, *wrath* really would seem like the best description of what is motivating God's behavior toward them. To repeat a point from chapter one, there are theological problems with the idea that God could be motivated by an emotion such as anger (even though anger may appropriately *accompany* an action from God). When God presses the truth on people, his ultimate goal remains people's ultimate flourishing. But the point I am making here is that, when God repeatedly presses the truth on a person who is resisting that truth, God's pattern of action will *seem* as though it is motivated by emotional outbursts of anger, or wrath.

After all, to the person who is resisting the truth about some moral flaw he has, he will not acknowledge this moral flaw. This truth is not something he believes. Perhaps somewhere in the less-than-fully-conscious recesses of his brain he will have some lingering awareness of his fault, which he won't openly admit to himself. But his dominant belief remains: "I am an innocent party here. I am not deserving of the trouble I'm experiencing. If others think I need to learn some lesson from all this, *they* are the ones who are misguided!"

For the person who persists in refusing to acknowledge the truth about himself, others who have a different viewpoint will be the unreasonable ones. Any external trials that God allows or causes will seem nonsensical and cruel. They will appear to have no possible point to them. Any promptings of the Holy Spirit will seem like *untruth*, like someone's pursuit of an unjust cause, like someone trying to push illegitimate guilt on him.

These promptings from God will of course persist, given the assumption that God will keep prompting people to acknowledge the truth until they have decisively rejected every avenue through which God can prompt them. In actuality, God is like a parent who cares desperately for a wayward child and is pursuing every possible avenue, no matter how drastic, in an attempt to help the child come to her senses. But instead of God's persistence seeming like the supportive efforts of a patient parent or friend, God's pattern of pressing the truth on her seems like the actions of an unreasonable, if not irrational, maniac. Again, in our eyes (the eyes of self-deceptive spiritual blindness), God would be the one insisting on some untruth about us, refusing to consider another viewpoint.

For people resolute in rejecting the claims God is making against them, they may naturally ask themselves why God won't simply let it go and drop his pursuit of them. After all, if another human continued this kind of pursuit behavior, we would view it as a clear example of harassment. As to the motives of the other human, these motives could seemingly only be explained in terms of some kind of misplaced anger, some kind of vindictive attitude that had consumed the other person and made him utterly unreasonable. In finding a phrase that best describes what God's persistent pressing of the truth on us will *seem* like if we continue to resist it, we really could not find a better phrase than "God's wrath" or perhaps "God's fury."

The Perceived Injustice of God Taking Up the Cause of Others

To make matters even worse, it will not only seem to those resisting God's truth that God is preferring his own desires to ours. It will also seem that God is preferentially treating other people, prioritizing their concerns over our own. As discussed in earlier chapters, truths about our moral character involve how we have treated God and other people. If we are to take our place within the heavenly community, we must own up to the truth about how we have affected other people through our misdeeds. Willful mistreatment and sins of omission must all be acknowledged and made right, if our relationships with others are to be perfected.

There is a strong theme throughout Scripture of God taking up the cause of those who are oppressed and neglected. At times, along with God's assurance that he will take up this cause, his instructions are for us to resist the attempt to play the role of repaying those who have wronged us. For instance, Paul quotes Deuteronomy 32:35 in writing, "Do not take revenge, my dear friends, but leave room for God's wrath, for it is written: 'It is mine to avenge; I will repay,' says the Lord" (Romans 12:19). Of course the promise here is that God *will* act in wrath, that he *will* avenge. Similarly, in Isaiah's prophecy of God's judgments on the nations, he declares, "For the Lord has a day of vengeance, a year of retribution, to uphold Zion's cause" (Isaiah 34:8). Continuing this theme, "According to what they have done, so will he repay wrath to his enemies and retribution to his foes; he will repay the islands their due"

(Isaiah 59:18). Again, in a particularly chilling declaration using the image of a winepress:

> I trampled them in my anger
> > and trod them down in my wrath;
>
> their blood spattered my garments,
> > and I stained all my clothing.
>
> It was for me the day of vengeance. . . .
>
> I trampled the nations in my anger;
> > in my wrath I made them drunk
> > and poured their blood on the ground. (Isaiah 63:3-4, 6)

But we must be careful in how we understand the term *vengeance* in these passages from Isaiah. People may use that term today to describe someone's enraged reaction to another person who has offended them. It may indicate a reaction like: "I'll get my own back on you, and you won't know what's hit you!" But the Hebrew word in these passages is a judicial term. It refers to a judge's just sentence on an offender. The word *redress* would be a more appropriate—and less emotive—translation. God is passing sentence on Edom and other nations for their oppression of Judah.

Yes, the language of God's judgment is violent. It is part of a vivid, extended picture of divine redress against Israel's oppressors. Obviously the picture language of a winepress should not be taken literally. But it is no less serious when read in terms of redress. God will need to go to extreme measures in pressing cruel and systematic oppressors to face up to the awful truths of what they have done.

Sometimes we must experience for ourselves what we have done to others in order to see the truth about ourselves in relation to them. This seems particularly so for those who reject the idea that they are the ones guilty for an unjust situation in need of redress. Indeed, we find in the Bible that God at times forces people to experience for themselves what they have inflicted on others. For example, in God's judgment against Babylon, he instructs, "Since this is the vengeance of the LORD, take vengeance on her; do to her as she has done to others" (Jeremiah 50:15). Again, "It is time for the LORD's vengeance; he will repay her what she deserves" (Jeremiah 51:6). For those who have oppressed others and who must therefore experience this kind of harm in order to understand who they have been in relation to others, the journey toward possible redemption will be a harrowing one. Combined with the pain that comes when one rejects this journey as appropriate (as previously discussed in this chapter), the journey becomes one of true torment. Seen in this light, the picture language of a winepress seems fairly apt as an image depicting God's redress in certain situations.

When redressing situations of one person's harm of another, God will of course always take up the cause of the victim. The laws given to the Israelites about how they should live together were designed to safeguard the poor and vulnerable in society (for example, Leviticus 25:8-17, 23-42, 47-55; Deuteronomy 15:1-18; Leviticus 19:9-10; Exodus 23:3, 6, 10-11). Accordingly, in the book of Isaiah we find a series of woes against the powerful and wealthy who have flouted these laws and taken advantage of poor farmers forced to sell their land because of accumulated debts.

In response to Judah's oppressive practices, God orchestrates events so that Judah becomes the one oppressed by others. In particular, Babylon becomes the agent of God's wrath against Judah. But Babylon likewise will need to experience the oppression they so gleefully inflict on Judah. They have "struck down peoples with unceasing blows, and in fury subdued nations with relentless aggression" (Isaiah 14:6). The king has dared to say, "I will ascend to the heavens; I will raise my throne above the stars of God. . . . I will ascend above the tops of the clouds; I will make myself like the Most High" (Isaiah 14:13-14). In short, Babylon has sought to rule over Judah with absolute and ruthless authority. God now declares that Babylon will experience what it is like to be ruled over in just this way (Isaiah 13:17-19). God will "stir up against them the Medes," whose ruthlessness extends to having "no mercy on infants, nor . . . compassion on children" (Isaiah 13:17-18).

Through this depressing cycle, God continues to hear the cries of the worker (James 5:4) and, in general, all those who are mistreated by others. God will of course always take up the cause of the victim, given his desire to bring fullness of life to all people. The problem, of course, is that we humans tend to welcome God's verdict when we are the ones judged to be the victims of mistreatment who can count on God's deliverance from others. But we are much less inclined to accept the verdict that others need deliverance from us. The biblical picture of humans is that we all inevitably play both roles.

If we are maturing in Christ, the truth about how we have fallen short in our treatment of others will be uncomfortable. Overall, though, this truth will be welcomed, as it leads to repentance, forgiveness, and restoration of our relationships with others. But if we are steadfast in rejecting the truth about how we have treated others, it will seem that God is unjustly taking the side of other people over against us. Their needs and feelings are being looked after; our needs and feelings are being ignored.

A thoroughly self-centered perspective, in which self-deception has warped our ability to see the truth about ourselves, inevitably leads to the perspective that we are the victim in cases where we have actually victimized others. Accordingly, when God takes up the cause of the oppressed and neglected, we will not see how we are in any way responsible for their plight. God pressing their claims against us will seem like an unprovoked attack against us: God unreasonably prioritizing their interests over ours.

The role of truth in this discussion must again be emphasized. When God takes up the cause of those who have been wronged, it is worth asking how God will take up their cause. That is, it is worth asking what exactly God will do to restore the victim. In a modern court setting, a judge may demand that the guilty party pay the victim some kind of financial compensation; and the guilty party may also be punished in some further way. But in the Christian picture of how people ultimately flourish, such things will not restore the victim. The redeemed in heaven do not need money, and they will not experience eternal joy because people they dislike are made to suffer.

As discussed in chapter six, the Christian picture of heaven is that people's relationships are perfected in love. That is what makes heaven a place where people experience ultimate flourishing. We also saw in that chapter that perfected relationships are only possible when they are built on honesty. What the redeemed in heaven need is for the truth of their relationships to be known: the truth of how they have affected others and the truth of how others have affected them. These truths must be acknowledged by everyone in the community. Otherwise, our relationships with one another can never be perfected. Anyone who *rejects* these truths about how all parties have affected one another simply cannot take a place within the community of perfected relationships in heaven.

What the mistreated and victimized need first and foremost from God, as he takes up their cause, is for God to expose the truth. In order to participate in the heavenly community, where healing and wholeness are found, they do not need to see their oppressors suffer. Again, there is no eternal joy and peace in that. But they do need for the truths about themselves and their oppressors to be exposed and acknowledged by one and all. (Of course, only God will know the full truth about how we have and haven't wronged one another, which helps explain God's injunction in, for example, Deuteronomy 32:35 and Romans 12:19 not to try to press this truth ourselves.) The sword of truth is what the persecuted need God to wield on their behalf against their oppressors, if the persecuted are to be vindicated and to take their place within a community that truly knows them and loves them. Even if the persecuted did desire retribution for retribution's sake, God could wield no greater weapon against the unrepentant oppressor than the truth.

Moving Forward

To summarize this chapter, God pressing on us the truth about ourselves is far from a mild rebuke. It actually amounts to the sharpest of weapons that can be used against us humans. This pressing typically involves painful external events, designed to prompt us with some compulsion to confront the truth about ourselves. Further, the internal presence of the Holy Spirit will be a continual and painful voice calling into question what we are trying to tell ourselves. Most devastatingly, God pressing the truth on us will undermine the general coping strategies humans have of dealing with any pain. The pressing of an uncomfortable truth about ourselves works directly against the human attempt to establish some distance between ourselves and the pains we experience.

For those who continue to resist the truth about themselves, God's pressing of the truth will be experienced as the kind of pain that cuts us to the heart like nothing else. Still, Christians can emphasize that the ultimate goal God has, when he presses on us the truth about ourselves, is *not* that we experience this pain that cuts us to the heart. Rather, his ultimate goal remains our owning up to the truth, repenting of it, and being restored to fellowship with him.

I have consistently talked about experiencing God pressing the truth on us as being painful, even a kind of attack on one's identity.

Interestingly, this need not be so. In fact, it might be experienced as the kind of faithfulness we associate with a mentor or close friend who has invested abundant time and care in helping us grow. Whether we experience God pressing the truth as God's wrath or as God's faithful care is, in the end, up to us.

8

THE CONNECTION BETWEEN
WRATH AND SANCTIFICATION

It is amazing how two people can look at the same object and see two very different things. Rorschach tests using splotches of ink illustrate this fact in a dramatic way. In everyday life there are so many events and conversations that we experience in a particular way, largely because we view these things through our own subjective lens. A person who continually "hears" sarcasm in other people's voices probably is pretty sarcastic herself. A person who finds that everyone around him seems obsessed with money or with power may well have an issue himself in one of those areas. Our interpretations of others' actions and words to us are inevitably filtered through our own subjective lens. This point goes a long way in explaining why God's actions will sometimes be described as wrathful.

Admittedly, this point will not explain all the painful aspects of experiencing God's wrath. As discussed earlier, God's acting in wrath will typically take the form of God allowing or causing painful external events to come our way. Yes, God's actions in such cases are intended to prompt us toward repentance. But the painful external events themselves are just that: they're painful! Still, the way we experience this pain, the way this pain affects our overall state of mind, is largely up to us.

I have emphasized that God's acts of wrath involve God allowing or causing a painful event to come our way, as a way of pressing on us some uncomfortable truth about ourselves. As a side note, throughout these discussions I am not at all suggesting that the pain we experience in life is always or necessarily God's judgment on us. Suffering in our world is by no means tied directly to a person's spiritual state. Certain characters in the Bible suffered precisely because they were faithful to God's calling: for example, Naboth, Jeremiah, and of course Jesus. Indeed, Jesus warned against assuming that some instance of pain or misfortune—such as a person being born blind (John 9:1-3) or people dying when a tower collapses (Luke 13:4-5)—can be traced to the sufferer's particular sins. In this chapter I am continuing to explore only those pains that are in fact the result of God pressing on us some uncomfortable truth about ourselves.

It is also worth noting the complications in knowing whether one really is experiencing God's wrath at a given point in time. A single event in life may have many contributing causes. For example, suppose Joe is fired from his factory job for repeated, angry outbursts at coworkers. Is this God's wrath on him? That is, is God as a last resort pressing the truth on Joe about his issue with anger, after repeated, gentler attempts to help him deal with his anger? Well, perhaps. But perhaps Joe's firing is God's protective hand over him, shielding him from an increasingly toxic situation at work. Or, perhaps his firing is due to a vindictive manager who has been looking for an excuse to scapegoat Joe and blame him for the factory's overall dysfunction.

Conceivably, all three elements might be at work, contributing to the outcome. Perhaps God is using the firing to press on Joe the truth about his anger issues. And perhaps God also intends this firing to be a divine means of faithful care and protection of Joe. And perhaps the manager's sinful, free choices are part of the causal story that results in the outcome. Events in life again often arise from multiple, contributing factors. God sometimes uses these events, sometimes orchestrates these events, and sometimes works with human free decisions, both virtuous and sinful. I emphasize that I am not tackling in this book the question of how we can discern whether a given, painful event in life is God's wrathful act of pressing the truth on us—or whether the painful event is a result of some other factor. I am instead simply offering a description of what kind of action God takes when he acts in wrath: specifically, it is a pattern of pressing on people some uncomfortable truth about themselves.

In chapter six we saw how this ongoing pressing of the truth can seem like an attack on our identity and on our very coping mechanisms, an attack that cuts us to the heart like nothing else. This is the key point: it can *seem* like such an attack. As to whether we experience God's pressing of the truth as a painful attack, this really will depend on how we respond to the truth with which God is trying to confront us.

PLACING OURSELVES UNDER GOD'S WRATH
OR UNDER GOD'S SANCTIFYING PROCESS

The process of facing up to an uncomfortable truth about ourselves will involve some amount of pain to anyone who experiences it. But I mentioned briefly in the last chapter that, if a person is maturing in Christ, this pain will be of a limited kind. It will be uncomfortable, but overall this uncomfortable truth will be welcomed. The context of this pain—again, for the person maturing in Christ—will be one of repentance, forgiveness, and restoration of our relationships with God and others.

It is helpful to think about how the process of sanctification occurs for us. This is the process of having our character transformed over time into the likeness of Christ so that we are able eventually to participate in the community of the redeemed in heaven, where there is no sin. We can develop some positive character traits through habit, as we respond appropriately to the Holy Spirit's prompting to care for neighbors, to comfort the sick, to reach out to the marginalized, and so forth. Still, much of our growth toward Christ's likeness will only take place by the power of God: as God changes our desires, patterns of thinking, emotions, and so on. In keeping with God's gift of freedom to us, God will change us over time as we choose to renounce the life of sin and ask him to change the parts of us we cannot change for ourselves.

So one crucial step in this process of sanctification will be our owning up to the truths about ourselves. Suppose we do own up to our moral flaws, then renounce them, then receive forgiveness for them, then have them removed over time by God. There will initially be some sting when we are forced to own up to some moral flaw which we previously were unable or unwilling to admit to ourselves. But as we are forgiven and begin to overcome this moral flaw, experiencing better relationships with God and others in the process, we will be grateful for God's original act of pressing the truth on us. It has made a new life possible for us. We more and more will welcome the future work that God must do to make us fully transformed so that our relationships are perfected in love.

The Christian saints throughout history testify that a deeper, more mature relationship with God involves coming to see more and more of those aspects of ourselves that must be renounced and transformed, if our lives are truly to conform to the likeness of Christ. This process can be one of overall joy, even though each new realization of an aspect of our selfish disposition may bring a tinge of painful lament. To those who respond properly to uncomfortable truths about themselves, the overall process of growth will bring with it abundant life. God's persistence in pressing these truths on us will—again, for the Christian saint—seem like the patient faithfulness that a beloved friend would offer: a friend who speaks the truth in love, a friend who is working toward the goal of our own full perfection and eternal joy, a friend who will spend as much time and effort as the task requires.

Quite another experience, of course, will await us as we resist the truths with which God confronts us, as discussed in the last chapter. But it is worth emphasizing once again that the intended goal of God's acts of wrath is people's long-term flourishing. In order to flourish eternally one needs to be reconciled fully to God and to others in relationships grounded in a shared recognition of the truth of who we all are. God's acts of wrath are one way—one drastic way of last resort—God has of prompting us to acknowledge the truth about who we are in relation to him and others.

As we saw in the last chapter, the book of Isaiah is one place in the Bible that emphasizes the way in which God's wrath is a response to sin. It is a contingent response that God stands ready to abandon whenever the people under wrath repent and turn from their patterns of sin and self-justification. Although the people in Isaiah are claiming that God is withdrawing from them, God presses the point that, no, it is they who have walked away from him. Yet, God extends the invitation he has always extended: to restore them and be reconciled to him, if they would only turn to him.

As a general Old Testament theme, even when God "in furious anger and in great wrath" thrusts Israel "into another land" (Deuteronomy 29:28), there is the promise that when the people "return to the LORD your God and obey him with all your heart," then God will "restore your fortunes" (Deuteronomy 30:2-3). As for other nations, as we have noted above, "If at any time I announce that a nation or kingdom is to be uprooted, torn down and destroyed, and if that nation I warned repents of its evil, then I will relent and not inflict on it the disaster I had planned" (Jeremiah 18:7-8).

In the New Testament as well we find expressions of wrath as prompts to repent, with God enabling a way out for those who turn to him. For example, recall Paul's admonition in 1 Corinthians 5:5 is to "hand . . . over to Satan" the unrepentant church member. He follows this instruction with the explanation, "for the destruction of the flesh, so that his spirit may be saved on the day of the Lord." (Paul seemingly intends that a period of exclusion from the church community will bring this person to repentance and so restore him to the community of faith.)

We find in the New Testament the full extent to which God is willing to sacrifice, to suffer, in order to provide a way out for people. (Hints at this suffering occur in the Servant Song of Isaiah 52:13-53:12.) Christ makes a way for all people to escape the pattern of sin, a state in which God's attempts to sanctify us are experienced as attacks from an enemy. Through Christ, enmity with God can be replaced by participation in God's very life.

The juxtaposition of Christ and divine wrath is a key theme in Paul's writings. In the structure of Romans, the warning of God's wrath (Romans 1:18) follows immediately the announcement of justification through faith (Romans 1:16-17). God's opposition to people's sin exposes them to wrath. But as I have argued throughout this book, a thorough analysis of divine wrath doesn't allow us to equate wrath with vindictiveness. Rather, divine acts of wrath are always for the purpose of prompting repentance, as a necessary step toward fullness of life as one is reconciled with God. Christ makes it possible for our repentance to lead in fact to reconciliation with God.

The Christian tradition has always agreed that Christ's atoning death and resurrection make reconciliation with God possible. Christians have sometimes proposed different models of the atonement in terms of how exactly this reconciliation is achieved through Christ's death and resurrection. But the takeaway point is that Christ does absorb the costs of our sin, making reconciliation with God possible through him. Paul emphasizes that Christ is the way of deliverance from wrath. He draws a clear line between those who are freed from wrath through trust in Christ (Romans 5:9; 1 Thessalonians 1:9-10; 5:9) and those who remain under wrath because they refuse God's merciful outreach to them (Romans 2:4-5; Ephesians 2:3; Colossians 3:5-6).

Importantly, we place ourselves under God's wrath by a refusal to respond to God's promptings, which are part of an intended process of our sanctification. To those who acknowledge the truth about ourselves and our need for Christ, we will receive God's promptings for what they are: acts of mercy and care. But Paul talks of those, by contrast, "who are self-seeking and who reject the truth and follow evil." For such people, "there will be wrath and anger" (Romans 2:8). Again, a key point is that people *place themselves* under God's wrath.

Equally, people can place themselves under God's process of sanctification, leading to final salvation. God's prompting with the truth comes to all of us. Whether we experience it as wrath depends on us. Each individual encounter with God's prompting can be appreciated as an uncomfortable but nonetheless necessary part of God's process of conforming us to Christ's image. Or that individual encounter can be experienced as an unnecessary assault on the picture of ourselves we are trying to cling to. When we resist an individual prompting us to acknowledge the truth, God of course must orchestrate a subsequent—and perhaps more forceful—prompting in his ongoing effort to help us come to our senses. In this way God's prompting becomes, to the person who continues to resist him, a pattern of increasingly pressing the truth on us. The key point I have been making here is that we place ourselves under this pattern of God's forceful pressing the truth against us. That is, we place ourselves under God's wrath.

Paul is by no means the only New Testament voice juxtaposing wrath and acceptance of Christ. The Gospel of John offers the context for remaining under God's wrath: "Whoever believes in the Son has eternal life, but whoever rejects the Son will not see life, for God's wrath remains on them" (John 3:36). But Paul is perhaps unique in the way he emphasizes that the fallback position for all humans is God's wrath. That is, all people—apart from the lifeline Christ provides for us—are stuck in a pattern of rejecting God's truth, which places us under God's wrath.

Paul's point here makes sense when we remember the narrative in Genesis of how God's response to Adam and Eve's first sin was to remove his special protection and blessing from our experiences of giving birth and working the land (Genesis 3:16-19). As we have seen, God's wrath is primarily expressed in terms of God showing people what life is like apart from his protection and blessing. There is a clear sense in which humanity has been living under God's wrath since the fall.

But it is not merely the fall of Adam and Eve that, for Paul, makes us universally under God's wrath. Paul reminds his readers in Ephesians 2 that "you were dead in your transgressions and sins" (Ephesians 2:1). How many people have fallen into this state? The answer is that "All of us also lived among them at one time, gratifying the cravings of our flesh and following its desires and thoughts. Like the rest, we were by nature deserving of wrath" (Ephesians 2:3). Happily, those who have accepted Christ can say with Paul that in his mercy God has "made us alive with Christ even when we were dead in transgressions" (Ephesians 2:5).

Paul refers to all of us as "children of wrath," a Hebraism meaning deserving of and liable to wrath. By nature we are in this state. That is, in ourselves and apart from Christ, we are all positioned under God's wrath. The Old Testament law doesn't provide a way out; it only "brings wrath" (Romans 4:15). That is, it accentuates this condition we are in, showing all the more clearly just how many ways we all have fallen short in our relationships with God and with one another. For Paul, *wrath* describes the condition of humanity apart from Christ. People are "separated from the life of God because of the ignorance that is in them due to the hardening of their hearts" (Ephesians 4:18). Once again, by suppressing the truth about who God is and about who we are, we place ourselves under God's wrath. We place ourselves in the position of experiencing God's truth as an angry outpouring instead of as a faithful prompting.

John's language in the book of Revelation draws special attention to the constancy of God's character in offering redemption, even while we humans may experience God's work in widely different ways. John points out that the prophesied "Lion of the tribe of Judah" has turned out to be a slain Lamb (Revelation 5:5, 12). Jesus of course reshaped our thinking about power, overcoming sin and death through his own sacrifice. True power is not coercive power. Rather, true power is creative love, through which God is able to transform fallen creation and redeem the world.

John retains this image of Jesus as the Lamb, even when he turns to the subject of God's wrath. We end up with the paradoxical language of "the wrath of the Lamb" (Revelation 6:16). The work of the Lamb was to sacrifice for us and to open up the invitation to join Christ in loving and serving others (again, the key to our own long-term, ultimate flourishing). But this invitation will not seem like good news to the person who is hardened in self-seeking pursuits. Such a person, blind to the truth about what she needs to do in order to find true happiness, will reject the offer of the Lamb. In John's depiction, those under God's wrath will be running for cover from the Lamb and calling out, "Hide us!" (Revelation 6:16).

But why the need to run and hide from a lamb? There is nothing inherently terrible about any action a lamb could perform, nothing that would be experienced as terrible by any and all people. Indeed, those who serve God will run joyfully to the wedding supper of the Lamb (Revelation 19:6-9). John's language brings out the point that God's intention for humanity remains their salvation. The "wrath of the Lamb" does not signify some sort of contradiction in the nature of the Lamb. Rather, for those who reject God's invitation to join him in relationships of self-giving love, the wrath of the Lamb is what they will inevitably experience if they will not partake in this love. As John Sweet puts it, "God must be experienced either as love or as wrath. . . . The Lamb . . . must appear as disaster to those whose horizons are bounded by this earth."[1]

In this section I have described our response to God in very simple terms: God communicates truths to us, and we experience them as either God's wrath or God's sanctifying grace, depending on our willingness to embrace these truths. In practice, this process is anything but simple. God's communication to us can take innumerable forms. It is typically mediated through our culturally formed languages, traditions, and expectations. Moreover, our ability to process God's communication to us can be affected by all kinds of life experiences—whether uplifting or traumatic. Only God can possibly sift through the unfathomably complex array of issues needed to discern whether particular people have been living up to the light they have had, to use a phrase from John Wesley.[2] In this section I have made only the generalized point that God's act of pressing the truth on us will ultimately be experienced by us either as a loving pursuit of our sanctification or as a wrathful pursuit of our ruin.

THE FINALITY OF ENDING UP UNDER GOD'S WRATH

I have emphasized repeatedly that God's expressions of wrath are not vindictive or emotional outbursts aimed at the punishment of

---

[1]John Sweet, *Revelation* (London: SCM Press, 1979), 145-46.
[2]John Wesley, "On Faith," in *The Works of John Wesley* (Grand Rapids: Zondervan, 1958), 7:197.

unrighteous people as an ultimate goal. Rather, the ultimate goal of any action associated with divine wrath is to prompt repentance, so that eventual reconciliation can take place. However, the Bible does contain a theme of there being a finality to God's wrath. That is, it seems that some people will eternally place themselves under God's wrath. Questions naturally arise about the sense in which God's wrath can be an eternally lasting response from God, if the people under God's wrath have decisively rejected God. If God's wrath really is intended as a prompt, then why does it continue even when people are past the point of being able to be prompted?

As an initial point, I readily acknowledge that the Bible does seem to indicate that some people will be eternally separated from God. Although the Old Testament picture of the end times is fuzzy, there are nevertheless hints in it about a final separation for some people. For instance, God remarks to the prophet Jeremiah, "In vain I punished your people; they did not respond to correction" (Jeremiah 2:30). Jeremiah is sent to warn Israel that they are continuing to walk into disaster. But God notifies Jeremiah that "When you tell them all this, they will not listen to you; when you call to them, they will not answer" (Jeremiah 7:27). In the end, their condition will be that "Truth has perished; it has vanished from their lips" (Jeremiah 7:28). With this decisive, final rejection of the truth God has tried to press on them, Jeremiah's only recourse will be one of mourning. God tells him that, at that point, "Cut off your hair and throw it away; take up a lament on the barren heights, for the LORD has rejected and abandoned this generation that is under his wrath" (Jeremiah 7:29).

In the New Testament we get clearer references to a final separation from God, which provides the primary support for a Christian doctrine of hell. The eternal life available through Jesus seems clearly to come in contrast to an eternal separation from God. I should say at the outset of this discussion that I am not arguing for a particular view on the fate of those who are eternally separated from God. There is some debate among theologians about whether God will keep alive for eternity those who have decisively rejected him. The alternative to eternal existence is so-called annihilationism, the view that at some point such people will cease to exist in any form. My goal here is not to engage in this debate. Rather, I will use the term *hell* to indicate the life and experiences of any person who has decisively rejected God and who is thus genuinely separated from him. Whether these experiences have a limited duration after one's earthly death or continue for eternity is a discussion for another time and place.

Back now to the question of how we should think of people in hell as under God's wrath, given that they have decisively rejected God. How does this connect with the idea that God's wrath is a prompt to repent? The answer is that, for those in hell, God does not persist in pressing on them the truth about themselves. But this is because God does not need to. Or perhaps it's better to say that there is no room for God to press the truth. The truth is being fully experienced.

Consider the following question. When God prompts someone to repentance with those actions we associate with divine wrath, *with what* is God prompting them? The answer, as we saw in chapter six, is that God gives them some foretaste of what life apart from him is like. In hell, people experience fully what life is like apart from God. On the view that God's wrath is a matter of pressing on people uncomfortable truths about themselves and their relationship to God, then there is a sense in which God no longer acts in wrath. That is, he no longer actively seeks to press on people the truth about themselves.

Yet, there is also a clear sense in which people in hell do remain under God's wrath. Consider the question: For those in hell, what is the truth about who they are in relationship to God? The answer is that they want nothing to do with God's invitation to join in the community of self-giving love. Those in hell will be in a state of spiritual blindness in which their hardened commitment to self-centeredness has made God's invitation seem like repellent news, not good news. People in hell experience the full truth of their character. That is, they experience the full implications of who they have chosen to be in relation to God. So there is a clear sense in which they can be described as having eternally placed themselves under God's wrath. They have fully become the kind of people who experience all of God's past and present actions as acts of wrath instead of as acts of loving care and faithful prompting.

On this understanding of hell, God is not actively doing anything to cause people pain. The pains of hell will be the natural consequences of life truly apart from God. Christian theologians have always agreed that there will be torment experienced by anyone in hell, owing simply to the fact that one is separated from God. Modern Roman Catholic philosopher Peter Geach summarizes this point: "God is the only possible source of beauty and joy and knowledge and love: to turn away from God's light is to choose darkness, hatred, and misery."[3] Similarly, Karl Barth remarks, "The enterprise of setting up the 'No-God' is avenged by its success."[4] Christian theologians have *not* always agreed on whether the torment in hell also includes God's active retribution, over and beyond what people are already experiencing from life apart from God.

Geach is among those Christian thinkers who view the pains of hell as entirely the natural consequence of life apart from God, who again is the one source of love, laughter, joy, and so forth. Geach comments, "God does allow men to sin; and misery is the natural, not the arbitrarily inflicted, consequence of sin to the sinner."[5] The alternative to Geach's position is to suggest that there is something

---

[3] Peter Geach, *Providence and Evil: The Stanton Lectures 1971–2* (Cambridge: Cambridge University Press, 1977), 138.
[4] Karl Barth, *The Epistle to the Romans* (London: Oxford University Press, 1931), 51.
[5] Geach, *Providence and Evil*, 138.

of value, something good, about God devising an extra form of punishment for people in hell, over and beyond what they are naturally experiencing apart from him. Consistent with the discussions of this book, I do not think any good case can be made for this suggestion.

Perhaps the motivation for the suggestion that hell includes an extra form of punishment is that the biblical imagery associated with hell seems more severe than merely living out the natural consequences of life apart from God. The biblical imagery of hell is alarming and at times downright horrific. In the book of Revelation John draws from judgment scenes in Joel 3:13 and Isaiah 63:2-6 in presenting a vivid, if grotesque, picture of people heaved into a "winepress of God's wrath." When trodden, "blood flowed out of the press, rising as high as [a] horse's bridle for a distance of 1,600 stadia" (Revelation 14:19-20).

If my suggestions in this chapter are right, what is being depicted in Revelation is the natural consequence of choosing life apart from God. Just how bad would this be? Keep in mind that, in this earthly life, those who resist God—even stridently so—will still benefit in a variety of ways from God's continued care. For instance, they will benefit from being members of communities here on earth where they receive at least some measure of loving care from other people, who themselves are following God's example of loving service in at least some ways. Even if their backs are stridently turned to God in this earthly life, they continue to have a variety of connections to God, the source of love, joy, and peace.

But genuinely to be separated from the sole, ultimate source of love, joy, peace, laughter, good will, unity, contentment, camaraderie . . . ? To be in a state in which *none* of these things are experienced? A person in such a state would be in the most pitiable of situations. Life would inevitably be one of uninterrupted loneliness, bitterness, conflict with others, and abject misery. The language of the Bible is often picture language, particularly in an apocalyptic book such as Revelation. How should the worst possible situation for humans—separation from the source of all well-being—be depicted in picture language?

In the last chapter, I noted that the image of a winepress doesn't seem inappropriate to describe cases in which a merciless oppressor on earth is forced to experience for himself what he has done to others. That discussion was in the context of how it might be severely painful for some people to be confronted with the truths of who they are. We can now add that all people in hell will experience the inevitable results of having decisively chosen to remove themselves from God, the sole, ultimate source of all things that make for genuine human well-being. Surely the picture of a winepress is not harsher than the "mere" natural consequences of experiencing life truly apart from God.

Admittedly, the picture language used in such places as Revelation seems to have a strong emotional component to it. I have argued that divine wrath, on careful analysis, is not motivated by emotional outbursts of anger or vindictiveness (even though righteous anger may *accompany* acts of divine wrath). In defense of my conclusion, I emphasize the need to look not only at the picture language of Revelation. It is also important to look at passages such as the following from the Gospel of John, which I have noted before: "Whoever believes in the Son has eternal life, but whoever rejects the Son will not see life, for God's wrath remains on them" (John 3:36). The contrast here between God's wrath and eternal life suggests that wrath is envisaged as the negation of all that eternal life implies. The focus is not so much on an emotional reaction from God but rather on the absence of divine life in those who reject the Son. Paul also contrasts the wrath of God with eternal life (Romans 2:7-8), as well as contrasting it with salvation (1 Thessalonians 5:9), justification (Romans 1:17-18; 5:9), and membership in the kingdom of God (Ephesians 5:5-6).

While not ignoring the emotional component to various biblical references to divine wrath (which are found most vividly in the picture language of apocalyptic literature from the Old Testament and Revelation), I stand by my overall analysis of God's wrath. To be in hell is not to have aroused God's anger to the point where he is "fed up" and therefore decides to abandon further avenues to restore us. Rather, following John Wesley, I affirm that God "offer[s] salvation to every creature, actually saving all that consent thereto, and doing for the rest all that infinite wisdom, almighty power, and boundless love can do, without forcing them to be saved, which would be to destroy the very nature that he had given them."[6] Although there is no point at which God *abandons us because of* his anger, we can nevertheless use our God-given freedom to place ourselves eternally under God's wrath by decisively rejecting his offer to participate in the fellowship of self-giving love.

I mentioned in chapter three that there is a sense in which we can speak of God as reaching a tipping point when he decides to act in wrath. But this just amounts to saying that, among the various strategies God has for prompting people toward repentance, God may decide at a certain point that the only effective strategy is to press on us uncomfortable truths about ourselves. Consistent with the arguments in this book, all God's strategies are for the ultimate, benevolent purpose of drawing people to himself.

The tipping point of God's wrath shouldn't be understood in terms of God reaching a point where he is so angry that he turns away from us. We turn from God, but never vice versa. Yes, God might recognize the tipping point at which we have decisively rejected him. This would amount to recognizing that we have refused every type of overture from God that could eventually lead to repentance. (Such a state would

---

[6]John Wesley, "Predestination Calmly Considered," in *The Works of John Wesley* (Grand Rapids: Zondervan, 1958), 10:235.

be the counterpart to the state of the redeemed in heaven, who have decisively rejected sin. Being fully sanctified, they cannot possibly sin, since every type of sin holds absolutely no attraction for them.) At such a point, we could rightly speak of God "abandoning" us—in the sense of having to leave us to our own devices, given that there are no avenues left for God to prompt us. But the main point I am making is that eternal separation from God shouldn't be thought of in terms of God reaching his tipping point and deciding to pour out his wrath on us in a decisive way. We make choices that lead us irretrievably to experience God's benevolent prompting as pointless acts of vindictiveness. We place ourselves under God's wrath, whether eternally or in this earthly life.

GOD'S WRATH AS BOTH FUTURE AND PRESENT

It is interesting to note the connections in the Bible between God's wrath seen as future judgment and as present reality. John the Baptist asks his hearers: "Who warned you to flee from the coming wrath?" (Luke 3:7). The background to this question lies in the expectation of the coming Day of the Lord, referred to by various Old Testament prophets (Isaiah 13:9; Amos 5:18-20; Zephaniah 1:14-18; 2:1-3). This was to be a time of decisive judgment when evil would be wiped out. Although these prophets were warning of times of crisis that were imminent in their own day, in the following centuries the conviction grew that there would be a final day of reckoning, for which all must make themselves ready. John's conviction is that this Day is now imminent and will be decisively inaugurated by the one for whose coming he is paving the way (Matthew 3:11-12; Luke 3:16-17).

Paul also speaks in terms of a future, final judgment, warning those who are unrepentant: "You are storing up wrath against yourself for the day of God's wrath, when his righteous judgment will be revealed" (Romans 2:5). This expectation of an ultimate judgment

when God's wrath will be at work is also evident in Romans 2:8; 5:9;
1 Thessalonians 1:10; 5:9. Jesus as well speaks in terms of a decisive
time in the future when God will judge the world (Matthew 12:36-37;
25:31-46; Luke 12:8-9; 16:19-31; John 5:28-29).

Consistent with the idea of a future wrath, John the Baptist exhorts
his hearers to repent. John's preaching about the coming wrath has
the potential to protect people from it. But the implication is that, if
the hearers don't heed it, their opportunity at some point will be gone.
The ominous association with the coming wrath is in large part because the time for possible repentance will have passed.

This theme of finality makes sense when we consider the Christian
view that each individual person at some point will have his or her
final destiny set. One will be in eternal fellowship with God or will be
eternally separated from him. Globally, the second coming of Christ
will mark the consummation of human history. There will be end
times and a final settling of accounts. People separated from God will
have placed themselves eternally under God's wrath.

At the same time, the relationship between the future and present
aspects of God's wrath is not one of neat separation. Paul makes it
clear that God's wrath is at work both within the course of history
and at the final judgment. The wrath experienced on that future
day—the wrath that people are "storing up" for themselves—may
already be experienced in the present by those who are hostile to
God's purpose in Christ. Paul can say of those Jews who played a part
in persecuting Christ and his messengers: "The wrath of God has
come upon them at last" (1 Thessalonians 2:16). Paul does not merely
warn of what *will* happen. He also believes that God's wrath is in
some ways already being experienced by these persecutors of the
early church. (Seemingly, Paul viewed God's wrath as being experienced at least in part through a series of political upheavals and
famines occurring at the time.)

In this way Paul is like an Old Testament prophet, viewing God's wrath as manifesting itself in natural and political disasters. Of course, Paul continues to warn of a future, final judgment in which there will be a confirmation of people's alienation from God. But the point I am presently emphasizing is that, for Paul, this alienation is already experienced by those who are refusing God's love as offered through Christ. God's wrath can only be thought of as both future and present.

Likewise, in John's Revelation God's wrath is viewed in the context of the end times. The image of the winepress represents final judgment (Revelation 14:19; 19:15). Other references to wrath are also associated with a heavenly announcement of final judgment (Revelation 14:10) or with human recognition that the final reckoning, the "great day of their wrath" (Revelation 6:17), is about to take place. Even so, like other aspects of the end times, this great day of wrath casts its shadow in the experience of history. Events such as the fall of Babylon/Rome, which are clearly within the historical sphere, are evidence of the wrath of God already at work (Revelation 16:19; 19:3). This "already but not yet" perspective is in keeping with John's conviction that God's future kingdom (Revelation 11:15) is already present (Revelation 1:9). The Christ who will finally come (Revelation 2:25; 22:7, 12, 20) already comes repeatedly in events of judgment (Revelation 2:5, 16; 3:3; 16:15).

Looking at the Gospel of John, it is characteristic of John's slant on the gospel story that he speaks not of a future, final expression of God's wrath but of wrath as an ongoing state that arises from refusal to respond to Christ. Just as eternal life is already the experience of those who trust in Christ, so those who refuse to believe in him are even now choosing for themselves the experience of alienation from God (John 3:16-21; 5:24). Once again, with reference to God's wrath there is not a tidy distinction between history in general and the final period of history. The whole period of history since Christ's death and resurrection is God working out his victory and the full establishment of the kingdom of God.

FREEDOM FROM WRATH

A main theme in this book has been the way in which God will persist in exposing the truth about people's moral character. In this chapter I have discussed how people's responses will determine whether this process leads to experiencing God as sanctifying friend or as unreasonable attacker. The truth from God awaits all of us. God does not offer anyone freedom from the truth. But there can nevertheless be freedom from God's wrath. Given my emphasis on God's wrath *as* a pressing of the truth, it might be natural to ask how a person could have freedom from one but not from the other.

The biblical narrative certainly affirms that Christians can experience freedom from God's wrath. We read that "God did not appoint us to suffer wrath" (1 Thessalonians 5:9) and that through Christ "shall we be saved from God's wrath" (Romans 5:9). Building on my overall analysis of divine wrath, freedom from divine wrath can be understood in the following ways.

God's truth will persistently be directed toward all people. The result will either be our entire sanctification or our decisive rejection of all the avenues through which God can prompt us to own up to the truth. Again, the exposing of the truths about us will persist. But for those who acknowledge this truth, God's exposing the truth to them will no longer be experienced as God's wrath. It will, once again, be experienced more like the persistently faithful—even if at times uncomfortable—acts of a friend who cares about our long-term well-being. Freedom from wrath thus includes freedom from an inaccurate picture of a vindictive God.

When God exposes the truth to those who acknowledge it and respond appropriately, God merely needs to offer the truth. I have used the term *pressing* to indicate the manner in which God will need to confront people repeatedly with the truth, if they continue in the pattern of willfully resisting it. This pressing of the truth brings with it the particular pains of being undermined in our attempts to cope with our trials by distancing ourselves from them. Freedom from wrath includes freedom from the particular pains of having our preferred identity continually undercut.

The pain of being under God's wrath is not only the particular pain of being confronted with uncomfortable truths about ourselves. There is also pain, more generally, from the natural consequences of life apart from God. But there can be freedom from the inevitable results that follow from rejecting the truth about ourselves, God, and others. We can be freed from a fate of eternal separation from the one ultimate source of love, joy, peace, laughter, and everything else that comprises the good life for us humans. We can be freed from having to partially experience this separation as we lead our lives right now.

Finally, it seems right to say that we can be freed from God's emotional anger directed toward us. Drawing from the discussion of chapter one, an emotion such as anger cannot serve as the ultimate explanation of why God would perform the pattern of action of pressing the truth against us. Nevertheless, God's righteous anger may still accompany this pattern of action associated with God's wrath. By accepting and responding appropriately to the truth about how we have related to God and to others, we are freed from God's righteous anger inhibiting our relationship with him.

In sum, there are a variety of ways we can think about being freed from God's wrath, consistent with the description of God's wrath I have offered in this book. We are never freed from God's work in exposing the truth about us, himself, and others. Indeed, it is this persistent work of God that makes our full sanctification possible, so that we are able to participate in the heavenly community of perfected relationships. But we can be freed from anything that should cause us fear. Whether we are freed is up to us. "The Spirit and the bride say, 'Come!'" (Revelation 22:17). But to take advantage of the abundant life God offers, as a responsive step we must own up to the truths God shows us about who we are in relation to him and others.

Is God a God of love *and* a God of wrath? In a sense, yes. But not in the sense that God's wrath could ever compete with God's love. God's wrath and God's love are not twin, equal pillars within the character of God. God's actions toward us are consistently and thoroughly loving. He invites all people into a loving relationship with him. Because this relationship must be built on truth, God will do all he can to help us acknowledge the truth. If this means he must press the truth on us in sometimes drastic ways, he will do that. He is that committed to our long-term good. God at times is a God of wrath precisely because he is a God of love.

SCRIPTURE INDEX

Finding the Textbook You Need

The IVP Academic Textbook Selector
is an online tool for instantly finding the IVP books
suitable for over 250 courses across 24 disciplines.

ivpacademic.com